T0194068

FREEDOM
WITHOUT
LIMITS

FREEDOM
WITHOUT
LIMITS

The Autobiography of Phyllis Fernandez

PHYLLIS FERNANDEZ

WESTBOW
PRESS®
A DIVISION OF THOMAS NELSON
& ZONDERVAN

WestBow Press books may be ordered through booksellers or by contacting:

WestBow Press
A Division of Thomas Nelson & Zondervan
1663 Liberty Drive
Bloomington, IN 47403
www.westbowpress.com
1 (866) 928-1240

Because of the dynamic nature of the Internet, any web addresses or
links contained in this book may have changed since publication and
may no longer be valid. The views expressed in this work are solely those
of the author and do not necessarily reflect the views of the publisher,
and the publisher hereby disclaims any responsibility for them.

Any people depicted in stock imagery provided by Getty Images are
models, and such images are being used for illustrative purposes only.
Certain stock imagery © Getty Images.

This book is a work of non-fiction. Unless otherwise noted, the author
and the publisher make no explicit guarantees as to the accuracy of
the information contained in this book and in some cases, names of
people and places have been altered to protect their privacy.

Scripture taken from the King James Version of the Bible.

ISBN: 978-1-9736-4009-7 (sc)
ISBN: 978-1-9736-4008-0 (hc)
ISBN: 978-1-9736-4010-3 (e)

Library of Congress Control Number: 2018911116

Print information available on the last page.

WestBow Press rev. date: 10/3/2018

*To My Parents, My Siblings,
My Husband, My Children,
My Grand Children and Friends
who are the reason for this book.*

Whosoever shall say unto this mountain, Be thou removed and be thou cast into the sea: and shall not doubt in his heart, but shall believe that those things which he says shall come to pass; **he shall have whatsoever he says.** What things soever you desire, when you pray believe that you receive them, and **you shall have them.**

MARK 11:23-24

CONTENTS

ACKNOWLEDGEMENT

This book is dedicated to my precious parents, my precious siblings, my precious husband, my precious children and my precious grandchildren. I owe my love and gratitude to each of you for standing with me through life's journey. Thank you, for your love and patience with me. Each of you have taught me great things in life. You have contributed much to my life. Life would have been so empty without you. I want each of you to know, how precious you are to me, and how thankful I am to God for each of you. You are the reason for the birth of this book. If not for you, I would never have had a story to write. God has given me a complete life with you. I am so happy and proud to be a part of you. Nothing will ever stop me from loving you. I cherish my life and memories with you.

Yours forever;

Your Daughter, Your Sister, Your Wife, Your Mother, Your Grandmother and Your Friend.

Phyllis

ACKNOWLEDGEMENT

CHAPTER ONE

The Reason For This Book

CHAPTER 1: THE REASON FOR THIS BOOK

*M*y earnest desire in writing this book is to Honor God, with Thanks Giving, for all that He has done for me in my life, and bring Glory to His Name. If not for this very purpose, I would not be writing this book.

I want to take you through my life's journey, and encourage you, how God's Amazing Power can touch you, transform you and mould you to the person, He chooses you to be. I Pray that every heart be touched and inspired by reading this book for The Glory of God. There is nothing impossible with God. He takes the meek and make him the king.

I am Thankful to God for showing me, the way to the Truth. He has done amazing things in my life. He has been there all along beside me, carrying me through, when many times I felt alone, in the lonely roads of my life. Yet there was always this inner strength in me which made me stronger and bolder, each time I encountered challenges. I had failed many times to recognize, that it was from God. Now that I recognize it, I want to share my happiness with this world, knowing, how you can become an overcomer, and find your freedom with true joy and peace in Christ. This is one of my favourite scriptures. Philippians 4:13 - I can do all things through Christ, which strengthens me.

It's only God, who can take you through, and make it through. Triumphant over your tragedies, Victorious over your failures, Strengthened from weakness, Joyful from grief and sorrow, bold- and confident from the fear of lack, insecurity, and intimidation. This is the driving force behind me to write this Book. I wanted to write a testimony of my life to inspire others. How I overcame my obstacles and found my freedom in God and Christ our Savior with The Power of The Holy Spirit.

Life's roads have taken me to many paths of ups and downs. I know, what it is to be joyful, happy and content, as well as unhappy, discontented and miserable. Through all of this journey, the most valuable lesson I learned is, " You are; who God says who you are; and not the summary of other's opinions. You are in-charge of your Life and your Destiny, and it's all about what you make of it," Knowing who you are in Christ, and seeing yourself as how God sees you through your imperfections.

You are not the summary of other's views, opinions, and suggestions. Who you are; what you can become; what you can achieve; what you are capable of; or what you can accomplish; is not for others to decide. Do not let others choose your dreams, visions and destiny, nor allow them to steal or destroy them. You are in-charge, you take control. Let no one steal your Joy, your Visions, your Dreams and your Passions. Embrace them, and pursue after them. Take charge, and take control. It's your life;

it's yours to take and make it happen. God has declared you a champion already.

You can rise above all your limitations, and fly free like an eagle, with a smile on your face, when you know how much God loves you and wants to set you free. Free from every bondage the devil throws at you. Free from struggling to be perfect, free from struggling to please others. Free from disappointments and discouragements. Free from your imperfections. Your total freedom and peace comes only from God. The world will only point their finger at you, reminding you of your imperfections, your wrong doings, where you went wrong and how wrong you were. What you should and should not have done, what you could and could not have become, where you should and should not have been. Decades of my life, I wasted, not knowing the truth. It was all people pleasing and disappointments.

Sad to say, certain cultures and beliefs can push you to the darkest roads of your lives. You become the cause of family misfortunes. At least that's what some believe. They talk about it over and over again; during family gatherings, during misfortunate times, when tragedy strikes, and so on. Unfortunately I became a victim of such beliefs. My parents never intentionally did any wrong. But again, they became the victims of such beliefs through friends and neighbours. It happened when I was born. My Dad lost his business and there was a financial struggle. Things were difficult. Friends and neighbours kept saying that the fourth girl brought my parents misfortune, which was me. I heard them speak about this over and over again as I was growing up. My parents were just repeating what others were saying, not knowing, how bad of an impact that was having on me. I remember listening to them and feeling sad for my parents having to go through difficult times because of me. It bothered me a lot. No one knew what was going on inside my mind. I did not question either, but accepted, I was an ill-fated child. When things went wrong in the family, my little heart knew it was all because of me. I suffered silently. Years went by; I went through many emotional roller-coasters. Never knew or understood God's plan and purpose in my life.

Only when The Power of God touched me, I realized that I did not have to struggle to live. Life became easy and breathable to me. Life became comfortable knowing how much God loves me, and He overlooks my imperfections. I am not who others say who I am and I do not have to live up to the expectations of others. I am who I am in the eyes of God. He created me and He Loves me. I need to live only to His expectations. Nothing else matters to me anymore. In my heart, I was consoled that I was no more that ill-fated, misfortunate child. God's perfect love set me free.

CHAPTER TWO

My Childhood

CHAPTER 2: MY CHILDHOOD

I was born and raised in an average family, to wonderful parents, who loved me, cherished me, trusted me, and brought me up to the woman I am today, along with my four siblings. Our parents taught us the values of Love and Respect from a very young age; in the family, in the school, and in the community. They took us to church every Sunday, visited our schools regularly, and also disciplined us when required. This is the norm in Asian culture. There was no abuse, although I went through some emotional trauma in my childhood, through some family members; which I carried into my adulthood. It bothered me for decades. Only when I knew the Lord personally, and His love for me, I was able to get over it, and forgive them. I did not discuss about this to anyone, even to my parents, thinking it might cause family division. Just recently, I mentioned about it to my youngest sister, while we were having a discussion about these family members. God's love can get us through any situation. His forgiveness towards us enables us to forgive others.

Our parents were well known in the community for their generosity and love towards others. My Mom was Mom to my neighbours as well. Well that's the type of culture we were brought up. All our neighbours were aunts and uncles. That's the way we were supposed to address. It was safe growing up. The whole community kept a watch on each other and their kids. If we do some mischief away from home, the neighbour aunt or uncle were also permitted to discipline us. Every one trusted each other and lived in harmony. Children were protected by all.

Growing up was fun. We were loved and protected. The whole neighbourhood could be trusted. There was no anxiety or fear in our parents, to know where their kids were playing, or whom they were playing with. It was for sure a trusted and protected community. What a Blessing it was to grow up in such an environment. It was total freedom. Freedom from the fear of being abducted or abused like it is these days. How I wish those days would return, so our kids and grand kids could enjoy that freedom. "It takes a community to raise a kid," our elders say. Our doors were open on all sides from the rising to the bed time. No intruders or thieves came by. The neighbour kids and the family kids along with their pets played together in and out of homes and even ate dinner together.

We had scheduled study time, play time, prayer time and supper time, every day. There were no late nights or hanging out with friends late. Dad usually checked our home work after work, and Mom took care of household chores with the help of maids. We exchanged visits with families and friends on occasions. There were, no drinking, smoking or foul language. We were observed with table manners, courtesy, respect, politeness and decent language. This was norm in everyone's upbringing. We accepted that way of upbringing. There were no complaints from us, since this was norm in every family. It may sound weird for this generation. But those were indeed golden days, and how I cherish them.

I grew up as a good religious girl, same as my parents. We were not aware of that relationship with God. I followed the good examples of my parents. Was kind, compassionate and helpful to others. Helped with chores at home when my Mom had health challenges and was always kind to others. I do recall a class mate of mine, (Her name is held to respect her privacy and protect her integrity.) who did not bring lunch any day, and I shared my lunch with her every day for years. If she is reading this book, she will definitely recognize me. This is the first time, I am ever mentioning about this matter. I did not even mention it to my parents. I am not boasting of my act of kindness here. I am expressing my gratitude to God for His Provision in my life, and the good attitude of generosity, that I learnt from my parents. I have heard my Mom say this, "When I do good for others, God will send help for my children, where ever they go." Sure enough, her children had favour where ever they went. Well, she did not quote directly from the Bible, but sure she knew the principles of the Bible, although was not familiar with the Bible. I did not understand those days, the principles of sowing and reaping. I automatically followed my parent's good acts of kindness. I never thought I was doing anything special. God was letting me sow the seed for my harvest. There was never a day in my life, that I did not have food.

I was also tough, when it came to defending my siblings, especially my youngest sister. Bullying was never heard of in schools. Seldom was it ever seen. One day, a class mate of my little sister made fun of her defective right arm, which was from birth. I was so distraught, and angry about it, that I punched that girl to the ground after school, until she apologised. I hid behind the wall, kept my little sister at a safe distance, and waited for that girl to approach. And I ran behind her and knocked her down. I can't believe I did that. Those of you who know me now, may say, it's not true. This book is my true, life story, nothing made up. No one knows about it till this day except that girl and my sister. There were no complaints either, Glory to God. I had strict upbringing and my parents would not have approved of that. Just not the disapproval, but whippings with it. Both my parents are not alive today to read my book and know of my little secrets. My siblings can, although in different parts of the world.

It's only for the Glory of God, that I am detailing my life story here. From the very first step of my life to this day, I can see The Hand of God in every area of my life. From my birth itself, according to the facts that I heard from my parents. I did not know then; but now I see and understand; God had a Divine plan and a purpose for my life. But the devil had opposite plans for me. I shall explain why. My Mom had a difficult labour with me. Although it was a highrisk pregnancy due to health challenges, my Mom chose to give birth at home with the midwife's assistance. That midwife was a close friend of our family, and my Mom was comfortable with her. And I chose to stay inside as breech with footling presentation, which was not good for Mom or myself.

The midwife had to rush my Mom to hospital, as this "precious one" refused to come out.

Finally, I arrived. The devil wanted to take my life, but God's Divine Protection was upon me and my Mother. Both our lives were at risk, the doctor said. But we were alive and healthy. Glory to God.

Today, I understand why God kept me alive. He had knitted me in my mother's womb and chosen me before the foundation of the world, with a Divine plan and a purpose. I know my destiny now. It is to serve Him with all of my heart and to let others know that, His Love can mend all brokenness, and we can have a joyful and peaceful life in Him. We do not have to live in fear and uncertainty. His love is so amazing. He is the restorer of our lives. Nothing is impossible for Him. He is our God of restoration. We just need to put our trust in Him, believe in his Promises, and receive them by Faith. All things are possible for him who believes. Every dead situation in our lives can be brought to life, through the power of the Holy Spirit who lives inside of us. We have God's Words, to council and guide us continually, and His Power to overcome the devil's tactics. God's Wisdom will enable us to have discernment and revelation knowledge. He will guide us to choose our paths. The steps of a righteous man are ordered by The Lord. And He delights in his ways. He will never let us stumble. And even when we stumble, He will pick us up. Glory to God. He is a faithful God.

CHAPTER THREE

Growing Up

CHAPTER 3: GROWING UP

I am always thankful to God for giving me a loving family, wonderful parents and siblings who I was raised with. I grew up to the expectations of my parents as a young woman, trying to maintain all values of life what my parents taught me. Yet I was not perfect.

I do remember the two very close friends I had. We were good students. Always trying to be on top, in class. Teachers were pleased with us. During the break time, we would hunt down any one who had said anything wrong about us and made sure they never repeated it ever again. I could sense my boldness from a very young age itself. The only complaint my teachers ever had in my report cards were, " Very Talkative in Class," for which I was always disciplined by my parents. I was pushed to be on top in class always, and if I came down a bit with my grades, I had it. The commends on my report card was reason enough for discipline. My parents would say; that I should not be talking too much in class; instead, be paying attention. Any Asian parents reading this book will know what I am talking about. The parents of my continent, always wanted their children to be on top, in grades, well behaved and good mannered and respectful. Anything contrary will not be tolerated. The children are expected to study well, and only study, study, study, and become great professionals or entrepreneurs. There was, no room for our own choices, if it were to be below the standard of their expectations.

Parents always provided with necessities. Part time jobs were never the norm for students. Parents normally took care of all school/ university expenses. I had never heard of student loans or credit cards in my early days. Even if it had to be to sell their gold, land or homes, parents of those days made sure their kids completed their school, went to university, got their degrees, and became a professional. I was one among those to be Blessed in that way. Not all would fall in the same category. I had seen many around me not so fortunate. I am eternally grateful to my parents for all their sacrifices. I thank The Lord always for giving me such wonderful, loving parents.

Parents have a great influence in the outcome of a child's future. A loving, caring home makes a child confident and strong. When the parents are trust worthy, the children grow up to be the same. When the parents are God Honoring, the children learn the same. When the parents are respectful and courteous, the children follow the same. A child is moulded so much in the atmosphere he or she is brought up, to become the person he or she is today. Parents, definitely have a great impact in a child's life and future. I cannot thank my parents enough for all that they have done for me, all the sacrifices they have made, and the heart aches they had gone through when we made some wrong or foolish choices. They made sure they were always there for us.

In good times and bad times. When we were sick or doing well. When we were sad or happy. They took care of us - whole. Spirit, Soul and Body. Lying or stealing were not permitted. Every day they checked our home work and school bags. I remember always exchanging my big new pencil for two small pencils. I thought quantity counted more than quality. My Mom never approved of that, I got in to trouble many times.

No one was allowed to hang out when it was study time, prayer time or supper time. All ate dinner together and prayed together. Home work and studies were done and checked. We kissed everyone good night before going to bed. They always tucked us in bed with a good night kiss.

Dad had worked for a Tea Plantation Company and worked extra hours at home doing some projects for the company, for extra income. He made sure the family was well provided. Mom never worked. But she always took responsibility, running the show. She handled all finances, did purchases, paid the maids, made sure her vegetable garden was well maintained; cats, dogs, chickens and cows were well fed and looked after. She made sure some money was put aside as savings, for our vacations, major purchases, like gold jewellery for the girls. There were no bank accounts. Money was always kept at home. She had a big container for coins, and the bills were bundled and kept in different rooms in different cupboards with secret cabins. The coins alone mounted up to a lot of money when we counted them. They were always involved in each other's lives and in the lives of their children. They never left us alone and went out partying or having fun. I remember sleeping with them even when I was 12 years old. When they felt we needed their company they always welcomed us. I don't ever remember them saying they were busy and not to interrupt. We were always well groomed. During the company's soccer match one day, one of the high officials of the company my Dad worked for, wanted to know who those kids were; well groomed and well behaved. He was surprised to know we were the kids of this ordinary civil work supervisor of the company, but well respected. I remember my parent's teachings, "Give respect and receive respect". Well, I believe it is true. When we are courteous and respectful to others, the same will be returned to us. And more over anything contrary to our parent's teachings had consequences.

Fruits and vegetables, and anything sweet were my favourites. I remember spending a good amount of time in our vegetable and fruit garden. There were oranges, beans, peas, carrots, garlic, peppers, spinach, corn, onions, pumpkins, radishes, tomatoes, chow-chow, tree tomatoes and so on. I ate lots of oranges, beans, peas, carrots and tomatoes daily. I loved them. My parents and siblings were amazed how much I could eat. My Mom warned me not to eat too much of raw vegetables, because it might upset my tummy. Glory to God, I think that's the reason I am so healthy today. The law of raw energy !!!. One thing she did not approve of me was, pinching all the tomatoes to check if they were ripened and pulling the carrots out, and burying back the leaves. She thought the birds were pecking on her tomatoes and some wild bandy goats were destroying her carrots, for a very long time. She kept traps for them, covered the tomatoes, with sack clothes, until she found out the truth one fine day, and I was warned not to do that again. We did not know then, the raw energy was so good for health.

On and off, bees made their nests on our tree tomatoes. When the season was ready, someone always came and extracted the honey for us. Basins of them at a time. We enjoyed the honey with bread. Licked up the honey comb too. Mom made delicious sweets with honey, which we enjoyed. Now I come to think of it, it was almost like the Garden of Eden, all natural.

We had two to three cows, which gave us fresh milk continuously, and enjoyed 3-4 glasses of milk every day. Liters of milk were sold to our neighbours, and Mom made her pocket money as well. Her business was in demand; as a trusted, unadulterated product was sold to them. She was a smart woman. A Proverbs 31 woman indeed. I have inherited that, although made some foolish mistakes at times, which ultimately made me seek God's Wisdom. Glory to God. Workers from Dad's company (He worked for), took cows out daily for gracing, and brought them back by evening. We enjoyed feeding them their meals in the evening. Mom had given them special names, and they responded so well to her. We had the cattle shed not far from home, and I remember my Mom spending so much time talking to them, patting them and kissing them and saying, "good night" to them. She made sure they were warm and comfortable for the night. Milk was extracted manually, morning and evening by the same person who took them out for gracing. We enjoyed carrying the full cans of milk to the kitchen for Mom to pour them in bottles for selling, and the rest were for our use. I don't remember our

Mom ever having to buy milk for us. She always had plenty left over and even gave it out for free when some couldn't afford it.

It brings tears to my eyes when I remember, how these cows shed their tears and refused to eat when our Mom went home to be with The Lord. I didn't know even cows could express their emotions to such extent. They felt the void. She was the first one to greet them in the morning and fuss with them. After the kids were sent to school, next were the cows for gracing. They felt her absence. It still amazes me. They even refused to come out of the cattle shed. Eventually Dad had to give them away, as he was not able to take care of them. They were my Mom's possessions. Priceless ones indeed. I have such clear memory of them. Their colours and even the spots on them.

The next members of our family were ducks and chickens. We had plenty of them in a large netted guarded fence with cage inside. My Mom always checked on the hens and knew how many would lay eggs that day. There was saw dust spread in the chicken and duck cage, for comfort, and warmth. We would watch chickens ready for laying eggs. Mom would collect them in a basket and bring them to the kitchen. My brother and I, when not in school, loved to do this; we rushed to collect them, pushing each other, and loved to play tricks on our Mom. She had a small basket for eggs in the kitchen. My brother and I made small holes in the egg and drank up the eggs raw, and left back the empty shells with the others. The next day when Mom was ready to use eggs for our breakfast she found some empty, and wondered why, and how the hens laid empty eggs. She was so innocently tricked, until after a very long time we admitted to what we did. She couldn't believe herself how badly she got tricked. We were not punished, as raw eggs were good for health she said. Chickens, Ducks and Eggs were another source of income. Mom never had to buy them for the family. All were organically grown and fed and there was no fear of unhealthy food. Our immune system was great. The Air and the Ground was with no pollution.

The tea plantations are in the high ranges, 5-6 thousand feet above the sea level with least amount of pollution. In fact, this birth place of mine called, "Munnar," has become world famous since some years, for its fresh air (Un-polluted), botanical growth and fresh water. It has become a tourist center now. The air is so clean and clear to breathe. It is a piece of land from The Land of Goshen itself. I never knew the value of it while growing up there. But now I see the value, and give God all The Glory. He Had Blessed me with everything from the very beginning of my life, which I failed to understand or recognize. I remember the mountains, the valleys and the small rivers where we used to play. Full with nature's beauty. Green pastures and flowers. The Splendour of His Majesty. We were so free from nature's corruption. I never realized I had freedom without limits even then. I remember climbing the mountain close to home after school with my siblings and rolling down the grassy hills to see who reaches down first. I did the same recently with my grand daughter here in the park, after decades. I enjoyed it so much, and had such fun with my grand daughter. My daughter-in love recorded us. It was amazing. I am still strong, and I can do all things through Him. Glory to God. Back to the story; We could hear Mom screaming on top of her lungs to get back home before getting hurt. Those days are cherished to eternity. We used to catch little fishes from the ponds and streams of rivers and bring them home in little bottles. We didn't have fancy fish tanks, so they had to remain in the same bottle. After few days, we let them free in the river. Didn't feel good to hold them back. Mom said not to limit their freedom.

I cannot go further without telling you about an interesting chicken story. In fact, it was the male. How he retaliated with my Dad. It is beyond belief. You remember I mentioned how our doors were left open on all sides from rising to sun set. Mom always left the chickens and ducks out of the cage for most day. They graced around home and in the yard. But few came inside the house, which Dad did not like, especially during his breakfast time. He did not want them to dirty the house. He used to chase them out. But Mom used to pamper them and had given specific names for them. She kept little chickens on her lap while sitting in the porch and had one or two on her shoulders too. Dad didn't want to be too friendly with them. One particular morning, this huge cock entered the kitchen door. He always ate well and was well built. My Dad tried to chase him out but he was bold and refused to go. So, my Dad took his umbrella and hit him and chased him out of home. This time he had to leave because he felt the blow. Dad went to work as usual. The day went by as usual. Kids got back from school. Dad's time was usually 5.30pm. He walked to work and back as it was close to home. We were playing outside our home. Chickens and ducks were having their leisure time as well. There was a path leading to our home separated by fence to our vegetable garden. We said "hello," to our Dad as he was approaching home. He smiled and wished us back. Then suddenly this male bird ran from near the fence and pecked my Dad's left leg. It was summer and he wore shorts to work. Dad had his umbrella with him this time too and hit him back again. He continued to fly back to Dad to peck him again. Dad had to use all his force and strength to finally get the bird out of his way. I have never heard of, or even seen such a thing. I still can't believe how a bird can harbour anger and retaliate. Our family will never forget that. Sad to say, his punishment was to get roasted for our meal. We did feel bad for the bird. But it was Dad's decision.

We had cats and kittens and dogs and puppies as well. It was fun. Mom used to stay awake during their birthing time. One time I witnessed a calf's birth. We cried along with the cow. It was too much to go through the whole process. Another time I witnessed a cat's birthing process. She carried the kittens one by one with her mouth to another safe and clean place which Mom had already prepared for them. I was the only one, bold enough to stay with my Mom and other care takers. My siblings were not so brave as me. Caring nature was in born in me. I paid attention to interact with animals and even with plants. I had the desire to become a doctor. Dad's income did not permit that. We had no student loans those days. The kids were not allowed to work part time either to support their studies. It was unheard of. I carried that tradition even to North America with both my kids, even with financial challenges in the beginning. We were taught, childhood should not be robbed of a child with extra burden, although child labour still exists. I never knew I was so Blessed. Now I recognize it and give God all the Glory.

Jimmy was our first dog. There were many after him. He is special, because he rescued my brother from death. I was not born yet, but my Mom told me the story. My brother was few months old, and woke up from his sleep and started crying while my Mom was taking her shower. My sister was beside him eating some food like cereal. She was just few years older. She kept stuffing food in to her little brother's mouth, thinking he was hungry and crying for food. The more he cried, the more she fed him until finally he was restless and choking. Jimmy sensed something was wrong, ran to the bathroom door barking and scratching the door violently. Since this was unusual, my Mom rushed out to check on the kids. It was life and death situation. The baby was struggling to breathe and restless. She found stuffed food in his mouth. Quickly she removed the visible food and tapped him up side down, and rescued him. Glory to God, he is still alive today and father of three kids plus two daughter-in-laws, and grand kids. My sister admitted to feeding him. The Hand of God was upon each of us, and is, up to this very day.

When I was a little kid, may be 2 years old, I went missing !!!. Wow, that was very unusual and unheard of. Our parents used to take us to sacred places like Mother Mary's Shrine, famous churches and so on, (Being Catholic). I Was born and raised a Catholic, until I met the Lord personally. I had always enjoyed our family trips. Mom's pocked money made up for our trips. Dad was the only worker. During the Mass celebration, while all were busy praying, I decided to sneek out secretly and go for a nap behind the alter. I really did fall asleep. Perhaps I wanted to get away a bit from the crowd and heat. Soon I could hear screams and crying, People running around looking for me. I didn't know how long I was there. All I knew was; I was awaken by the crowd and the noise. I think my Dad found me, comfortably asleep, behind the alter. Perhaps I was dedicating my life at the alter from that very young age!!!. All the screaming and crying came to an halt. They grabbed me, hugged me and kissed me. I was too precious to them. They couldn't be without me. The angels were protecting me, so no harm came near me. The devil tried to take me away from my parents. God's protection was hovering over me.

I graduated from high school with good grades, loved science, and hated maths. Scraped through for maths. Glory to God did not fail. Did not know then, to operate in God's wisdom. Then I would have confessed in line with God's Words. Today I am aware, and speak in line with God's Words and Bring to pass His Blessings in my life. I know I can have what I say. (Mark 11:23). I am thankful to God for His Word, and His Promises. I Went to college, chose science to be my main subject. Zoology was my favourite subject. Lived in hostel. Dad came and picked me home during vacations. During my vacation, my passion was to show my science talents to my family, especially my Mom. She was very proud of her daughter choosing to become a nurse, as she was a patient herself with diabetic/hypertensive complications which sent her to hospital many times. She spread the word to the entire town, that her daughter was going to become a nurse. I would ask our care taker to get me frogs, earth worms and cockroaches, to dissect and experiment. Although my family was nervous to watch me dissect these poor creatures, they were amazed at my courage and encouraged me. My Mom said I was a brave girl and that I would thrive anywhere. Sure, I did. Her confession made me thrive everywhere. I Decided to become a nurse. I had practiced giving needles to patients from my childhood. My patients were cotton pillows and my needles were broomsticks. Only thing; I left the needles behind, and my Mom had to frequently change our pillows.

Here is a great example of, "You can have what you say". Let me take you back to my early child hood and school age. Do you remember the nurse (Our family friend) who had to rush my Mom to the hospital to get me out, which I had mentioned earlier?. Well; I liked her a lot, admired her a lot, and called her "Nurse Aunty," from my childhood. And hung around a lot in and out of her clinic, playing with her son who was my class mate. She wore eye glasses and looked very professional to me. I kept saying to my parents, that I would become a nurse just like her when I grow up, and would also wear eye glasses. I thought it was cute to wear glasses. Little did I know that there was already an existing eye problem with me which my parents or myself did not know at that time. I was born Myopic, (Short sighted). In those days, there were no neonatal eye testing or any such routine testing. Everything seemed normal was deemed normal. I was a healthy kid. My parents had no concerns, as everything seemed normal. I thought, everyone saw the world the way I saw. I was not able to see the leaves clear on a tree unless I was closer to the tree. From far it looked like a green cloud. Could not see the leaves separate. I did not know there was something wrong, because I never knew the brighter side. I thought everyone saw the same.

Even in school, since I always sat in the front row, there was no problem to see or copy down from the board, where the teacher wrote. Then one day everything changed.

All things work together for good to those who love God, to those who are the called according to His purpose. (Romans 8:28). It was good that I talked a lot in class !!!. The teacher disciplined me and put me at the last bench one day, away from my close friend. It was the class test time. We were to copy down the questions from the board. All I could see was a white cloud on a black board. Nothing was clear to me. So, I asked the next student who sat beside me to show me the questions as I was not able to see clear. He did show me the questions and I was writing them down. The teacher knew it was very unlikely that I would copy down the answers from another student as I was one of the top students. She approached me and asked me what was wrong. All I remember was not answering her, but burst out crying. I did not cry because I could not see. I cried because I was embarrassed thinking I would be accused of copying down the answers, which was not true. The teacher took me aside and asked me what was the problem. My first reply to her was that I was not copying down the answers, but only the questions because I could not see clear. She was very kind to me and allowed me back to my seat and complete my test. She wrote a note to my parents and asked me to pass it to them. We had no home phone at that time, only the company phone. And surely no cell phones. My parents were shocked to receive this news. They took me immediately to the eye specialist. Got me prescription glasses.

The world had totally changed for me. I was in Awe. I had

never seen anyone or anything so clear in my life. The world looked totally different to me. I was saddened to know, this is the way everyone seen the world, and I was deprived of it. Yet I was excited with my new world. Could see a person's face clear from far and see each leaves clear on the tree. It was an exciting and emotional moment. I had to wear thick glasses. No fancy thin ones. I was so happy and enjoyed every moment of my life with my new world. My heart was delighted with my new world. I was, one happy kid. My parents took me for regular eye checkups. Each year the vision got poorer. My parents were concerned. They prayed for me always. I too prayed for my good vision. No one knew the scriptures. We had no Bible at home. Only heard the Priest read from it on Sundays. I was raised as a catholic. Did not know how to confess God's words. We accepted the negative reports what the doctor said and did not know how to reject it, and speak God's Word over it. Did not know sickness was a curse and it was not God's plan and will for our lives. Did not know how to put the devil in his place. All his manipulations, we accepted calmly thinking it was God's plan. We were deceived so badly. Not anymore. Glory to God. Thank you, Jesus. My parents took me to natural treatment centers, for my good vision, which had to keep me away from my school and studies, and I was not agreeing to continue that. So, had to discontinue the treatment.

The devil is a liar and father of lies. God's Wisdom has empowered me to discern the enemy's tactics. When we have God's Wisdom we automatically yield to His Word, and go by The Holy Spirit's leading. And it will always take us to victory. That is what I am enjoying now. Victory in Christ Jesus. The basic principle is, to put God first in our lives, and include God in our every day endeavours. Life without Him is dangerous. I have tried that many times, making my own decisions and ending up with failures and frustrations. I thought I was very smart and can handle everything very well. Yes, I did seek His council on major issues and decision makings. But on minor issues, I thought it was not required. Well, now I learned, in everything to seek His Council first. I will never try doing anything by myself ever again.

Seeking God's Council, Yielding to His Words, Obeying His Commands, Claiming His Promises and receiving them by Faith, will always bring us through any situations. There will be no room for regrets and disappointments. Because we have chosen His Will in our lives. The just shall live by Faith. We will never be put to shame. Instead of shame, He will give us Double Honor.

A heart of gratitude will always keep us humble. Self righteousness is pride and it is destructive. Resting in God's perfect Love gives us peace. We cannot earn His Love by our work. His Love is freely given to us. It's not on our merit points. There is no demerit points in Him. It doesn't matter, how many times we mess up, His Love never changes. His Love is eternal and His Mercy endures forever. All He asks us is, to simply believe in Him and follow His instructions. He will never leave us nor forsake us. His Promises are forever yes and amen. His Words will not return to Him void. But it shall accomplish what He pleases, and it shall prosper in the thing for which He sent it. His desire for us is to prosper in all things and be in health just as our soul prospers.

A grateful heart will not complain and murmur. God's Love

is so deep and wide for humanity, He sent His only Son Jesus to die on the Cross for us, so we can live freely. We receive His free gift of salvation, and forgiveness of our sins. Jesus' obedience to The Cross bought us Salvation. Not our works !!!. He took our sins and gave us eternal life. He took our poverty and gave us plenty. (Abundance). He took our sickness and made us healthy and whole. He took our shame and gave us double honor. This truth brought me to repentance. How could I ever repay such a Loving God. I sure had to put away my pride, arrogance, disobedience, ungratefulness, selfishness, bad attitudes, and self righteousness. I humbled myself to His obedience. When I realized His Unconditional Love for me, it began to change me. No more I had to do things in order to please people. My good works cannot earn His Love. His Love is freely given to me. I just need to trust Him and believe in Him and rest in His Perfect Love. I am not in fear of anything or anyone anymore. Why? Because His Perfect Love has casted out all my fears of imperfections. Someone else's opinion about me doesn't count anymore. They can say, think or do what they want. It doesn't bother me anymore. What is important to me is to know that God Loves me through my imperfections. I am in right standing with God because of Jesus. I am the righteousness of God in Christ Jesus. This life of mine, is different from all these years of pain and toil. I don't toil anymore. I am enjoying the "REST" in His perfect love. This revelation knowledge has brought me great peace and joy to my life. I live in Lavish Abundance of His Love. His Blessing and His Favor is upon me and my household all the time. I don't need to beg God for anything.

My Salvation came with The Blessing when I received Jesus as my Lord and Savior. The devil had blinded me from knowing The Truth. The devil kept feeding me with his lies and I had fallen in to his trap. He kept telling me," you are not good enough, you cannot do things right, you are a failure, you messed up again, what will others think about you, you are unlucky, that's all you can achieve, you are not smart enough, you cannot afford it, It's only for the rich and not for you, you are not beautiful enough, and much more." And I worked hard to be that person everyone wanted me to be. Toiling....Toiling....and Toiling, with self efforts. Thanks be to God for those who imparted me with the Wisdom of God. Life is so easy now. Not having to please anyone, but Him only, and rest in His perfect Love. There is so much Peace and Joy, and I am able to achieve so much more. Life is no more a struggle. It is so beautiful and wonderful knowing you are precious to God. No matter what, God Loves you unconditionally. He is longing to have a relationship with you. He is not with a stick to beat us down when we faultier, as the false religion teaches us. I always thought He was an angry God who was waiting to punish us when we made a mistake. What a false religious teaching that is. When I found out He was just the opposite, what a relief it gave me. I can breathe freely now, Glory to God.

CHAPTER FOUR

I Became What My Mouth Spoke

CHAPTER 4: I BECAME WHAT MY MOUTH SPOKE

Remember, Mark 11:23. You can have what you say. Let me take you back to my childhood once again. How I confessed with my mouth that I would become a nurse like that "Nurse Aunty," and would wear eye glasses when I grew up. Well that's exactly what I did. Wore eye glasses from grade 3, thanks to my talkative mouth which caused my teacher to discover my vision problem.

I was sure, and determined to become a nurse by profession. Got admission in one of the best teaching institutions in Southern India, Bangalore, which was associated with a Medical College. Started my carrier training, which was amazing. We had excellent devoted teachers. Four years went by quickly. Went home every year on short breaks. All the family members took up second opinion from their family nurse. I enjoyed being their medical mentor. Life took a bad turn for me during that period. Had to rush back home with the news that my Mom was seriously ill and was admitted to hospital. I remembered how with tearful eyes she said goodbye to me when I left home for my carrier training. Many fearful thoughts invaded my mind during my travel back. I did not know then, to declare healing over my Mom with God's Words. None of us knew the Word, and its Power. I got home; Dad took me to the hospital. Mom was already in diabetic coma. She couldn't talk to me, but knew very well her nurse daughter was beside her. Even with insulin drips, her blood sugar remained high. She was in diabetic/ septicemic shock with resistant bacterial infection from an unhealed wound, after a fall. No antibiotics had effect on her. She was resistant to all. Doctors had given up hope. We were made only to believe them those days, as the ones to write our destiny. We were not aware that we could take authority over our lives, lining up with God's Words, and change our destiny. What a tragedy to the ignorant ones. Sadly, we were one of them. Initially Mom used to respond to calls. But gradually she slipped into deep coma. The reason Dad took her to hospital was, when he found her one morning sitting in bed crying. She couldn't get out of her bed. Couldn't move her legs. She did not want to go to the hospital as usual, but had no choice.

Her condition grew worse, and had to be transported to a Major facility hospital. Throughout her last 17 days I stayed beside her. She always had confidence in me. I only took bathroom breaks. Everyone looked up to me for comfort, as I was the nurse of the family and the confident bold one. I was crushing inside, nowhere to turn. Had to remain calm and bold for my Dad and my siblings, especially my youngest sister who was 9 years younger to me. She was only 11 years old when Mom went home to be with the Lord. My Mom had always asked me to take care of her when she passed away. She never asked my older siblings. I have two older brothers and an older sister as well. I am the fourth one. I used to help my Mom with house hold chores and taking care of my baby sister whenever possible and required. My older siblings were away in college and at work. I was mostly at home, until I went away to college. I was very responsible, considerate, compassionate, and capable too. No wonder I chose the right career. My Mom always bragged about me, that I was a courageous and capable girl and that I would thrive anywhere. I believe, that is the key to my inner strength which took me through my life's rough roads later on in life.

CHAPTER FIVE

Life Without Our
Pillar Of Home

CHAPTER 5: LIFE WITHOUT OUR PILLAR OF HOME

*O*ur desperate days were fast approaching as Mom's condition grew worse day by day. I remember the scene so clear. It was our Mom's, "Good Bye" day, January 8th 1979, at 2.30pm. Our Grand Mother and I were beside Mom. She was gasping for breath. She was already on oxygen and many tubes. Dad and brother had gone to get her medicines from pharmacy. No free meds there. She took her final breath, the "Good Bye" breath. My Dad and brother could hear us screaming and crying as they were approaching the room. My Dad with hands full of I.V fluids and medicines was about to collapse. The kids and Grandma were screaming and hugging on to him. He lost his life-mate and children lost their mother. Her mother (my grandmother) lost her baby daughter, the siblings lost their little sister, friends lost their trusted and cherished friend, neighbours lost their beloved neighbour. Both our grandpas were long gone. Destiny was so cruel. My brother started pulling out the tubes, even before the nurses were to. He stated, "Leave our Mother alone, let her depart in peace without these tubes". Mom was the precious baby to my grandmother. She raised her, fatherless from her birth. My Grandpa went home to be with the Lord, when my Mom was born. It was too much for her to bury her little girl. Mom was only 45 years old. My little sister was brought to the hospital by our family friends; Mom's best friends. Others were on their way knowing her condition was deteriorating. Everyone arrived. Some got the news late, so did not make the trip to hospital, but were already waiting for us at home.

We had a new world to face now. A world without a loving Mom. She was a woman of integrity and loyalty. Very loving and kind. Everyone loved her and respected her. From young to the old, the whole neighbourhood called her Mommy. She was indeed loved by all. Mom was brought home for viewing. People were flooding from all over, apart from family and friends. She did not go to the morgue. We wanted her home. The front room was ready to receive her. The cats and the dog laid at the foot end of her bed. Would not budge. They had tears running down. The dog did not bark even at the strangers. They knew their Mom had left them. They did not eat for days. Mom had their special cookies in a cabin, which they would run to whenever Mom would open the cabin door. We tried opening it many times to get them to eat something. They just refused. It took days and weeks to get them to eat something. The cows felt the void too. They refused to get out of the cattle shed. They too had tears running down. I never knew cows could cry, missing someone. They refused to eat as well. When they had to be given away, they went with tears. Mom's absence was very loud to all.

Mom had a dignitary's funeral. She was not an high official. But in many people's heart she was one. Floods of people paid their respect. Floods of flowers. Our Grand Mother moved in with us which was of great comfort. Our aunts and uncles stayed with us for sometime. One of them stayed with us a little longer. Dad went back to work. One day he entered home calling out for Mom. It was emotional to all. I kept my word to my Mom. Paid more attention to my little sister. She continued her school from home. The older ones had to be back to their studies and careers as well. We missed Mom too much. Many continued with their visits. She was never going to be forgotten. Dad needed that comfort. She was his strength after God. My Dad was the bread winner, but Mom was the administrator. She ran the home-business very well. They were very close. Loving couple. Mom was the queen of home. We had to pick up the pieces from our shattered life. Life without Mom was not a happy one. We missed her terribly. Her laughter, her jokes, her love, and her cuddles. There was so much emptiness in our home, which no one could fill. Time would heal they say. But it took us a long time. We did not know to lean on His Word and His comfort. Even the chickens and ducks, dogs, cats and cows, felt the void.

We didn't know The Words then; God's Words; which would have comforted us. We didn't know to seek His Presence and Council, so we relied upon friends and family for comfort. The wound took a long time to heal. It was time for me to go back to continue my nursing education. I was sad to leave my little sister, Dad and my grandmothers. Our Dad's Mom was already living with us. My siblings went back to their destinations as well. All missed Mom, including the pets. Life was never the same for all of us. I graduated as a Nurse. The one who would have been the happiest and proud, was not there to witness it. Yes, from heaven she did indeed.

God sent a special person to my path. She was an Irish Nun, who was in-charge of the department that I worked. I was still grieving for my Mom. This Nun comforted me always, saying my Mom is rejoicing in heaven with no pain. She asked me, if I would rather have her beside me suffering or rejoicing in heaven with no suffering. It was difficult for me to accept my Mom's departure. This caring nun used to carry bananas and chocolates for me in her pocket to feed me if I had not taken my lunch break, caring for an ill patient. My food and break time was not important to me, if any of my patients were ill who needed me. If a patient needed urgent blood, and if not available, I would be the first one to reach the hospital blood bank to donate. Many of my co-workers did the same. Few of us had to be warned not to exceed the limits of donating blood, for our own health safety. We were young and strong; so, we thought we could just keep on donating. I remember one incident, when one of my patients were bleeding badly from her internal organs and had to have many units of blood, and the family couldn't afford to pay, I begged the blood bank to empty me as much as possible to save her life. The patient or the family had to pay for blood and medication. They warned me after my final two units of blood, not to return for a while. Many other hospital staff donated as well. God had ordained me as a loving and caring person and a nurse. For God's Glory, I am saying this. I was chosen and set apart from my very early age, from my mother's womb itself, which I did not recognize then.

After the mandatory serving period, at my school of nursing, most of my friends were going abroad to work. Middle East was the market then. I applied and was selected. Dubai or Bahrain was to be my destination. Dad's choice was Bahrain according to his friend's advice. I accepted my Dad's advise and went to Bahrain, was hired on contract by the government hospital. Before leaving, this Irish nun presented me with a little Bible and advised me to read from it daily at least a line. I obeyed her and did what she asked me to do. As a child while growing up, I had heard of nurses going to work in Canada. A little dream seed of Canada was already placed in my heart as a child. I do value now, visions and dreams, as they are inspired by God. I remember looking up to the aeroplanes in the sky and imagining one day to sit in a plane and go to Canada, and work as a nurse. At the same time, the devil had put a negative thought in my mind as well. I still remember those thoughts, "How could I, an ordinary child ever even think of that, it's not possible." I didn't know God's Words then. Neither did anyone speak them over me. Oh Lord, what a Blessing and Privilege it is to know your Word.

When I was leaving for Bahrain, I smiled and thought of my dreams of going to Canada. I considered it as a false dream and tried to forget about it. Little did I know of God's plans of prospering me in Canada, (My soul's prosperity). Bahrain did make me wealthy, but my soul did not prosper there. I enjoyed working there. The Arabs were kind and good. One thing I admired of them was their hospitality, and their habit of honouring their God in everything. They acknowledged their God in everything. I never did that those days. Yes, I honoured God and thanked God, but not in everything. It didn't come natural to me. I was a religious catholic, kept my faith, followed my parent's good advice, attended church regularly, worked hard to please God and others. I did not know about the relationship with God.

Looking back to my childhood days, I do recall a very important seed sowing time of God's Word in our lives. We never grew up with a Bible in our home. We heard the priest reading from the Bible on Sundays. But God always finds a way to sow His Word in to our hearts. Because my Mom had many health challenges, and had frequent hospital visits, she became a favourite of most of the hospital staff. Nurses, Doctors and other workers. My Mom always had a charming and attractive nature which brought many closer to her. Some say, that I have inherited her nature. Glory to God!!!. Because of this friendship, many nurses visited our home on their off days, and prayed with her and for her. They were Pentecostal. They read their Bible, clapped hands, sang hymns, and prayed with Mom. The kids were asked to join them, but we preferred to hide behind curtains and watch them and giggle at times, for which we were disciplined. They lifted up their hands and prayed with tears. It was something unusual for us. They visited my Mom frequently and prayed with her. My Mom enjoyed their prayers and presence. God was sowing His Precious Word, as seed, from early on in our lives. We didn't know, that was the true way of worshiping Him. Every step of the way God was working in our lives. We did not recognize it.

CHAPTER SIX

My New Life

CHAPTER 6: MY NEW LIFE

*L*ife in Bahrain was amazing. God had great plans for my life, and that's why He took me to Bahrain. I had enjoyed my carrier and my new friends. Lived in a hostel provided by the Ministry of Health. My Dad was overly concerned about me, as I had no family or known people around me. He was sad that I was alone. He used to write long letters to me giving me all the details back home, even 15 to 20 pages at times which made some friends of mine question me, asking if it was really my Dad's letter or my boy friend's letter. They did not believe me until I made them read his letters. They said no fathers would write such long letters. Well, God had given me special loving parents. I was afraid to have a boyfriend, which was norm to the good old Asian culture.

In the mean time, Dad was desperately searching for someone in Bahrain who could visit me so that I wouldn't be lonely. He wrote to our family friends in Dubai, if they knew someone in Bahrain to come and visit me. Dad's prayers were answered. They had their close friends in Bahrain. I was so Blessed to meet the most beautiful loving family in the world. Such loving and caring people. I had a home to go to. They visited me in the hostel, and from then on took me to their home on every off-duty days. I enjoyed their company. They did not do this just for me. Any one from their home town who were new to the country, they accommodated and fed them freely until they were settled well, even if they did not know them personally. Thank you so much, Pam and Dessy, for all that you did for me and my family.

This loving family was going to make history in my life. That was God's Divine plan. I did not know then; that I would be meeting my future husband there. I met many people in their house, as their home was warm and welcoming to all, including few bachelors. I was not looking out for anyone at that time, except for constant reminders from Dad which made me pray to God, asking Him to put my life partner on my path. It was during the same time, I was attending a charismatic prayer session from my hostel. They used to lay hands on our prayer requests and pray. My only prayer request was to show me my life partner. God was behind it all the while. My husband; the then bachelor, always wore a ring on his finger, when ever I had seen him at my friend's place, and I thought he was already a married man. My new friends and his family were close friends from the same town back home. I still was not looking out for any man. My Dad started sending pictures of eligible bachelors to me, constantly reminding me that, without Mom, he did not want to leave his responsibilities unaccomplished. And I was the next one in line to get settled.

During this time, my sweet friends took a vacation to their home town; and my husband's Mom, approached them and asked if they could find a nice girl for their son in Bahrain. They were close friends. Their answer was that; they knew a nice girl working as a nurse, who would be a good match, provided he stopped his wild ways. He was a hero of mischiefs then. God had great plans for him too.

After the vacation, my friends came back and gave me the news. Only then I confirmed he was not a married man. He just wore the ring for fun. To God be all The Glory, he was kept for me. Then, something in my spirit changed. God put a desire in my heart, to get married. I was still not looking out for someone.

Every two years we were given vacation with air fare. The time had come for my first vacation. I was all excited to see my family. Bought lots of gifts for everyone in the family and also for friends. My Dad and siblings greeted me at the airport. My heart was heavy as with others. There was a void in all our hearts. Mom's absence was so heavy in all of our hearts. I was comforted to be back home. Missed my Mom a lot. Dad did everything to fill in both places. He missed her so much too. The pets were happy to see me as well. It was good to be back home. Dad spoke to me about settling down, to get married. He had mentioned in his many letters as well. I was not ready. Was back to Bahrain again after the holidays.

The routine shift work at the hospital and life back with my adorable friends, started. Every time I went to their home, my future husband and few other bachelors were always there. I also continued with my prayer group every week, with the same request for God to put my life partner on my path. Then one day everything changed. My future husband approached my friend and asked if she could speak to me about our future. She conveyed the message to me and I agreed. We sat down together in their house and spoke. Just casual talk and he said he has had many friends, (Girls), who were nurses; and also that he was going on vacation; and if I agreed, he would go down and meet my Dad and family. I agreed with no further thoughts. I felt in my heart this was an answered prayer from God. Prayers do work.

He went on his vacation, went down to see my Dad and family, along with his two brothers, sister in law, and a friend. My family liked him alot. My grandmother fell head over heels for him. Coming from a large family of siblings, loving parents and grandparents, his loving heart was sensed by my grandmother, Dad, and siblings. They had no second thoughts. My Dad felt very happy and relieved. Finally, his prayers and desires to see his daughter getting settled had come to pass. He sure felt relieved, to complete his responsibilities. Dad informed me of all the news and he couldn't wait until the engagement date was fixed.

The groom arrived after his successful vacation trip, Promising his loving Mom, Grandmother, and siblings, that he would behave well, now that he decided to settle down. It was a happy time for me as well. From then on, we started hanging out together. Now I had more families to visit. His brother's and sister's homes, apart from my friend's home.They were all very warm and loving. But we spent most of our time in our friend's place. We did not miss church. I was taking guitar lessons those days; before I met my future husband. Apart from becoming a nurse, my childhood dreams had also included, becoming a singer and a taxi driver. God fulfilled those desires of mine as well. I sing now with my church congregation, Glory to God; and drive always. I was preparing myself to be the sober driver for my future family life. The designated driver after parties. Guitar had to be put away, as I was no more interested in it. Slowly the prayer group attendance came down as well. Continued to receive Dad's long letters without fail. Always with great parental advice and with all the home news. He never forgot to remind me of fixing the date of my big day. We had to heed, as parents and grandparents from both sides were waiting for the big day. Finally, after a year of getting to know each other; date for our engagement was announced. We decided to get engaged in Bahrain, and the following year to go down to India and get married. His Mom, Grandmother, and siblings loved me very much. His Dad had already gone home to be with the Lord. His Mom and Grandmother always advised him to be responsible. We got engaged with all of his siblings and our family friends around us. My new life began. We loved each other very much and continued our lives enjoying each other's company, our families and friends. I had to get accustomed to my new found life. A total different lifestyle from my upbringing. Lots of parties with alcohol, club visits, dances and so on. I was never raised in such atmosphere. My parents, siblings, or extended families never entertained such life style. They never drank, partied or went to clubs. I thought I had to please them. Never knew to take God's council. More over I loved the man God put in my path. So, there was no turning back.

The wedding date was fixed. Life with many late night parties continued. Birthdays and anniversary celebrations. I had no complaints and enjoyed life. But somewhere deep down I had questioned my life style many times. I ignored them. Nothing else mattered then. It was time for our big day. We went down together to get married. My Dad came to pick me from the airport. On our way home, I met my sweet new Mom to be and the rest of my man's family. Very loving people. Dad and my siblings had arranged everything for our wedding. I got my wedding dress and ring from Bahrain. Same with him, his suite and ring. We got married on 27th December 1984. Missed my Mom a lot. Everyone missed her. Went on a short honey moon trip, facing few challenges already. I thought that's the way life works. Didn't have God's wisdom to handle life. Just followed the crowd.

Our lovely lives continued. The first 2-3 years of our marriage kept us busy enjoying parties and fun life. Then we decided to complete our family. Planned to have kids. I remember praying and asking God to give us twins so that I don't need to go through another pregnancy, and desired only for two kids. Well God always answers our prayers and gives us the desires of our hearts. My Pregnancy was confirmed. I had this extra desire to eat a lot, along with morning sickness. I had these thoughts in my mind, may be its twins. My husband thought the same too, as they have family history of twins. And that's why I was always hungry. In the mean time, my pregnancy was progressing. I spoke to the doctor in the maternity department where I was working then. She asked me to come for an ultrasound. She did the ultrasound and confirmed I was right. We were having twins. I was so excited and called my husband to give the most exciting news. He was on top of the world. Very excited. The doctor gave me a copy of the ultrasound. Further scans showed they were both boys. I have kept all those records till today. Our twins are 30 years old now. Went home from work and both of us celebrated our twin's news. Informed families and friends. All were so excited. My pregnancy was closely monitored. Both of us spoke to our babies, and prayed with them daily. Didn't know the Word, but loving words from parents. I experienced weird pregnancy symptoms. I disliked ice cream which I used to love the most. Body weight was increasing, along with pregnancy complications.

I was asked to be hospitalized for close observation due to pregnancy related complications. Gestational Diabetes, High Blood pressure and excessive weight gain due to oedema, (swelling). They put me on a diet, and insulin. Had severe reactions to insulin. So, had to change medications and stricter diet. I was hungry all the time. My husband visited me every day. He sneaked in food for me on my request, because I couldn't tolerate my hunger. Being a nurse and being a patient are two different things. I was an honest nurse, but was not an honest patient. All my friends, the nurses and doctors took good care of me. I was progressing well.

One evening during the regular visiting hours, the water bag ruptured. My husband was beside me. I knew this was an urgent matter. So, I asked my husband to use the call bell. The nurses rushed to my bed side, seeming it was urgent, as I never used the call bell any time. I was anxious as our babies were premature. My husband was anxious too. Since the previous night, I was experiencing mild contractions, but I did not tell the nurses, all because I was not comfortable with the doctor on call and did not want to go in to the labour and delivery unit, under her watch. I was rushed from the ante- natal unit to the labour and delivery unit. I was well advanced in labour, already 4 cms: dilated. My husband was too worried, at the waiting room. Called his family. All came running. My labour progressed very quickly. The monitor showed one of the twins in distress. His heart rate was too high. Doctors and nurses were all- ready and waiting. They said I was one of the most co-operative patients. All I did was squeezing the mattress tight, and never screamed once. Amazing strength of God. I kept praying our babies would have no complications. Didn't know The Word then. Didn't know how to speak life over them. Thank God, I knew Jesus at least.

It was a Sunday, 29th of May, 1988; close to midnight, 11.30-11.34pm, Both our twins were born. Both were in Breech position just like their Mom. Healthy preterm handsome babies, looking just like their Dad. The first twin, (Alston), had cord around his neck wound tight few times, which had made his heart rate go high. God's amazing timing. Had I not gone in to early labour, we would have had a still born baby. What an amazing God we serve. Premature labour, was God's amazing rescue plan for our precious child. Neonatal specialists and the midwives attended to him quickly. Our second precious one (Aldon), took a while to come out. The doctor had a bit of challenge to get him out quickly. He did not cry immediately after birth, which ought to be, and I was a bit concerned. Finally, he cried. His legs were a bit twisted as his twin brother gave him not much space, while inside. I held my world for the 1st time in my hands. God's treasured possessions; the answer to our prayers. They had to be transferred to the special care neonatal unit for close observation. They were well taken care of. Because of the distress I was not able to breast feed them immediately. They were put on I.V fluids and Oxygen. Their proud Dad, uncles and aunts seen the twins before being transferred to the neonatal unit. I visited them early next morning. They were in the incubators. I touched them, talked to them and told them how much I loved them. Later their Dad visited. We wore gowns and masks and carried them. God's amazing gifts. We were the proud parents. We Thanked God for His amazing gifts. Our precious gifts from God.

I was doing well, except for the normal wear and tear, and lack of sleep. The twins had to stay back at the hospital for few more days. Had neonatal jaundice and photo therapy. (Light Therapy). Visited them frequently. They were on breast feeds and bottle feeds. The day came for them to come home. My sweet friends took me and twins to their home as they knew I would need help. Also, the home we lived in were under renovation with lots of dust which would not have been good for the newborns. Their Dad visited daily, and went home at night. After a month when everything was clear we went to our own home. My friends helped me with the twins a lot. We sent pictures of them to all our families back home. All were excited with the twins. Families and friends visited us almost every day. It was exciting and tiring time.

My Dad sent my little sister to help us with, soon as she competed her university. That was her first job. Taking care of our twins. She was of tremendous help. A great reward from The Lord. She did a lot for us. My husband was not a night watcher. So, I literally stayed awake day and night. As they were premature babies, close attention was required. I hardly slept for 1-2 hours a day. My husband went back to work. After 4 months, I had to go back to work as well. Thank God for my sister, who was more than a Mom to our kids. She took good care of them while we were at work. Our days were very busy. Its only God's amazing Grace and strength that took us through. No words can ever describe the gratitude we owe to my precious baby sister Marina, for all that she did for our precious kids and us. God is her rewarder.

Parties and late nights, still continued. Didn't know how to balance the new life. My husband could sleep through the storm; not so with me. I was an over alert Mom. Was afraid, babies would choke at night. People perish due to lack of knowledge. I was one of them whom the Lord had great grace and mercy upon. So, I did not perish. Literally slept an hour or two every day, in spite of the great help from my sister. We were excited and spent money without the wisdom of God. Soon it started affecting us. The main pay cheque had to wait until I was back to work. It was a challenging time, physically, emotionally and financially. The strain of life took a toll on me and our marriage. I felt I was working 24/7. No one knew; I went in to depression. My close friend said, I was not the same bouncy, bubbly person any more. Who would understand me? Silence was my best answer. I tried to cope with life with a brave front, with a smile. Life was not the same anymore. Families and friends visited, everything kept me busy; but I was sinking inside. Because I always put a brave front, no one could notice, what was really going on with my life. Life became a roller coaster. Our marriage was not the same any more. We were drifting apart. I felt betrayed and let down by life. I loved my precious children more than my own life. So, couldn't think of leaving them behind and going anywhere. I fought within, and struggled within. Had no one to talk to. Felt lonely and isolated. No one could sense anything was wrong. Post partum depression was unheard of in those days, to the non-medicals. No one would understand such things. Finally, a day came; when I couldn't cope any more. So, what happened next was unbelievable, even to myself. What I am about to say will shock my family and friends. The only person I disclosed this to; after many years, is gone home to be with the Lord. (She was my husband's youngest sister). I decided to end my life, taking my precious babies with me. I did not want them to suffer without their mother. I couldn't trust anyone to leave them behind. I battled with life and death for few days. The thoughts of going away, leaving behind my loved ones, especially my Dad, who sacrificed so much in life and raised me up, was unbearable. I was angry within myself. Hurt beyond description. Couldn't care less about anything or anyone else. My spouse could find another wife, after I'm gone; I thought to myself. But I knew it in my spirit, my Dad would burst his heart and die. I couldn't do that to him. So, I put off my plans, and asked the Lord to forgive me and give me thoughts of a new life. I asked him for strength to go through life and raise my kids with no shadow of my pain visible to them. My ever loving God sustained me, and brought me out of that fiery furnace, without a hair of mine being burned. He rescued me from death. His plans for my life and my children's lives were greater. I will never fall into the pit of satan's lies ever again. Satan came to steal, kill and destroy my family. He has no more access into my life, nor my family's lives. He has a restraining order, through Jesus' Name.

After four months of my children's birth, I went back to work.

I chose to do night shifts, so my children would not miss me much. My sister trained them up well and took good care of them. I would catch up a bit with sleep, play with the kids and be off to work, while they slept. The only peace I had was my children were in safe hands. I am eternally grateful to my sister for all what she did for our children. They call her "Anta," till today. And she calls us "Mamma, and Dada," till today along with our kids. We are thankful to God, she has been blessed with a great husband, and two wonderful children, who serve the Lord.

Days and months passed by quickly. Satan tried to rob my life again. It was summer of July 1989. My children were a year old. Summer in Middle East is extremely hot. I was driving to work on an afternoon shift. Was running a bit late to work, so speeded, hit a curb, went rolling with the car, and ended up side ways in the middle island of the two-way traffic, very close to the hospital where I worked. Since seat belts were not mandatory those days, I got thrown out of the car in the soldering heat, with my shoes and glasses flying off of me. But I stood up, blistering my feet with the heat of the tarred road. God sent his Angels and rescued me. To everyone's surprise, there was no traffic on both sides who could have smashed in to me. Neither did my car obstruct any traffic, as it stayed tilted in the middle island. Then I seen a van pulling in on the opposite side of the road. Two men came running out to help me, and said they would take me to the hospital. I asked them to take me to the very own hospital where I worked. They were true Angels sent by God. I could not get hold of them after. Those good Samaritans took me to the emergency department, and left. With all the excitement, happening, I could not take down their information, as I was bleeding all over with shattered wind shield glass pieces all over my body, making my white uniform look red. I was still giggling, feeling like a fool. No pain any where, except for the blood and blistered feet. The afternoon shift nurses went to the resuscitation room first, to take over the critical case, knowing the person in that wrecked car had to be there. When they saw the room was empty, they presumed that person is already in the morgue. This I came to know only later. As the nurses approached my cubic, they screamed and asked me, "Phyllis, What are you doing here, don't tell us, you were in that wrecked car." I giggled and said," yes." Then they said, "you are never going to die again, coming out of that wreck." That was a good confession, which I didn't know then. Then they started attending to me, first by pulling out the glass pieces out of my body, while they observed a blue finger on my right hand. X-ray showed fracture, and they attended to it. I did not even feel any pain. No pain anywhere in my body. My husband and family came by, soon after they were informed. I was still giggling, it was like something funny had happened. I was given time off from work. It took me more than a month to wash my hair properly, as the thin flakes of glass were still stuck on my scalp. Had to shake them off frequently. Rubbing the scalp was not possible. God rescued me from death with the power of His Blood. Satan failed miserably once again. God rescued me from every pit the devil had laid. What a loving, merciful Father. I was always grateful to God, but not to the extend I know Him today. He has done great things for me.

Time went by quickly. Twins were growing up fast. It was

time for school. Mother was anxious more than them. I was afraid they would be fearful and cry. Their first teacher was our very own family friend which put me at ease. I remember the day I drove them to school. I still had my uniform, straight from night shift. Left them in the class and stayed outside until they finished. The teachers said I could leave, but I didn't want to. I waited, in case they cried. It may sound funny to many, but not so with this Mom. I never wanted my children to hurt in any ways. Seems weared?. Not to this Mom !!!. Glory to God, my grand daughter started her school this year. I was tempted to do the same, but did not want to go against her parents. It was a bit challenging. Within few years my sister got married to a wonderful, Godly man, and moved out. Twins missed their Anta. But they visited us frequently.

One of their school days brought great fear in me. The house boy who used to pick them from the school bus stop, did not show up. So, they crossed the high way themselves and went into our neighbour's house. I was on day shift those days. When I reached home, I didn't find them. I panicked, ran out to see if they were playing outside. When I didn't see them, I became breathless with fear, and called our neighbour, and they joked saying they did not see my kids, while they were there. They did not know my state; I was about to collapse. I was screaming at my neighbour to ask their kids if they had seen them. Then they knew, my state and said to calm down, and that my kids were there. Instead of saying "thank you," I was shouting at my neighbour for scaring me. Later I came to my senses and thanked them and apologized. They were good Christians, fed my kids and kept them safe. When we left

Bahrain, they gave me my first KJV Bible and a small Bible for my kids, which I still treasure. I did not read the Bible then, but later in life I did. God always surrounded us with good people. I did not recognize, those great favours came from God Himself. This book will not end if I put in everything. I am just picking and choosing. I have always heard my Mom say, that she loved doing good for others knowing that God would send good people into her children's lives. There will always be help arriving for her children. She was so true.

Life took us through many roads. There were many ups and downs. Faced many challenges. Through it all God brought us stronger together. We had trips and vacations with kids. All the family members were very excited to see the twins grow. We dressed them alike always. Strolled them in twin pram. They were notable twins; everyone stopped by and admired them. They were the apple of our eyes and treasure of our hearts. Now our grand daughter has taken over that place. We love our grandson much too. As years went by, they did not want to be dressed alike. They celebrated their birthdays with parties at home, school, and with special friends separate. We were always surrounded by families and friends. Fun time, busy time, and stressful time. God's presence was always with us. Work and family kept us busy.

CHAPTER SEVEN

Decision On Our Future

CHAPTER 7: DECISION ON OUR FUTURE

*I*t was time for us to decide about our final destined place to live. Middle east was not our choice. Going back to India was not our choice either. My husband's brother and sister were moving to Canada. In the mean time, I already had papers ready to move to Australia with a good job offer, with family sponsorship. Put in application to Canada as well. I had already forgotten my childhood dreams of going to Canada. God was always in it. The hospital where I worked, did not want me to leave. I had God's favour every where I went. They even gave me a higher position and a raise in salary, so that I would stay. They always appreciated me as a sincere worker who could be trusted. I was sad to leave them as well. I was also confused at that time, didn't know what to do. To leave a good income giving job and go to a new country and start all over, was not an exciting thought. Didn't know to take God's council and make decisions. I did pray to God, but didn't know the Holy Spirit or how to rely on Him and not to be anxious. God's true wisdom came very late in life for me. Thanks, be unto Him, who is ever faithful even when we don't see it. I thought I was very smart. I thought God made me that way, and I was very proud of myself. Little did I acknowledge Him in everything. He was patient and faithful to me all the time. Now that I have come to know Him, I am a different person. I am nothing without Him. Everything what I am today is only because of Him. He is everything to me. He is my Saviour, my Deliverer, my King, and my Supreme Authority. Only in Him and through him I can function. I don't need to sort out my life anymore. He has already set my life and mapped out my path. This is so easy, just rely on him and move forward. He knows the end from the beginning. My heart is so much at ease now. Not afraid of failures, not afraid of being judged. I have His answers already; nothing but victory. He has purchased it all for me with His Precious Blood. What a Blessing!!!, to know the truth and live a peaceful life. God, I thank Thee; every minute of my life.

We made up our minds. Moving to Canada was our decision. (My childhood desires were being answered by God), which I was not paying attention to then; but now I know. Although my husband's younger siblings were in Australia, we thought, moving closer to the older siblings were wiser. We kept delaying our move until no further extension was given by the immigration. Both of us resigned from our jobs, kids out of school, packed and moved to Canada. It was a sad time for us, leaving all the comforts of established lives, and moving into an unknown land, to start all over again. We cherish the memories of Bahrain. In this land I met my husband, and in this land my adorable children were born. There are so many memories to cherish. The people were loving, trustworthy, friendly and helpful. We enjoyed everything in that beautiful pace. The saddest thing was to leave behind our pet. Bullet; our dog. From a puppy, he grew up with the twins. He always thought he was one of them. When ever I called out to my sons, (As Sannapets), he used to be the first one to come. The triplets; we would call them. He often slept between them during their day time naps. He was very protective of them. When my Dad visited us from India for the first time, he was over cautious of the kids, as if my Dad would harm them. It took him few days to really welcome my Dad. From then on, he was confident and left my Dad alone. We loved him and the kids loved him even more. The kids and us were extremely sad, to leave our pet behind. We had plans to bring him later to Canada, once we were settled. My sister and brother-in-love, promised to take care of him, to our blessing. Instead of him moving in with them, they moved in with him, so that he could live in his own surroundings, without being hurt further. It was a sad time for all of us. Thank God, He always provides a way.

CHAPTER EIGHT

The New Chapter In Our Lives

CHAPTER 8: THE NEW CHAPTER IN OUR LIVES

We said good bye to our family members and friends especially our pet and boarded our flight to Canada (my childhood dreamland) on April 2nd, 1996. Little did I even think at that time, that, God was fulfilling my heart's desires. It's only after some time, that I started realizing it. Our family members were waiting to receive us at the airport. Thank God, for family. It was still winter. The most exciting thing for us was to see the real snow for the first time in our lives. Kids were excited. We wanted to experience more snow. God always grants us the desires of our hearts. Within a day of our landing, one of the worst snow storms hit our province. It was one big excitement day for all of us. We stayed with my husband's older sister and family for two months, before we moved into our own place. They made snow man at the back yard, and the kids wouldn't want to stop playing in the snow. They were dressed for the weather, but still I was afraid they may fall ill due to the cold weather. I did not know then, how to confess God's Word over them and not to harbour fear. Thank

God, He has delivered me from all fears. Both my sisters-in-Love, took me for a long walk in the snow. I feared I would freeze. My husband stayed back. He enjoyed just watching the snow. I was really excited and happy, that I did not freeze, and enjoyed the scene. God's grace was sufficient to adjust our lives from plus 40-50 degree- c- to minus zero. God is so amazing.

Kids were enrolled into near by school. Our close friend Charlotte (We call her Charlie), helped us obtaining the required documents like health card and so on. Charlie and her family are very precious to us. We were friends from Bahrain itself. Her youngest son and our twins were born around the same time. The family members had to go back to work. We walked our kids to school, as it was close by. My friend would pick us up and take us to her home, and drop us back on time for the kids. She did a lot for us. Where ever she went on fun trips, she always took us with her and her family. We went to church on Sundays with our family. The catholic church. There was still a spiritual void in me. I started looking for more spiritual fulfillment. I was seeking for more of Him. After we moved out from my in-laws home, I was looking for a Spirit filled church. From the dry cleaners, I got a flyer with a Pastor's number. I called that number, and that Pastor picked us up to church. My husband did not come. He wasn't very happy then, of my visit to some other church with the kids. More over the kids told their Dad what they experienced; falling and rolling with the Holy Spirit's move. I felt uncomfortable too, since it was my first experience. It was a denominational church. I was warned by my husband, not to take the kids there any more. So, I stopped. But I never stopped looking for that fulfilling God, to fill my void. I knew too well something was missing. I continued to pray, asking God to show me the right church. The apartment we moved into was the right place.

One day, as I approached the building with my kids from school, I saw a smiling beautiful lady. We introduced ourselves. Our kids went to the same school. I remember the first thing I asked her. I wanted to know if she went to a Christian church; a Bible believing church; and if I could go with her. She was so happy to welcome me. The following day was Sunday, she had to go early to serve in the kid's kingdom. My kids and I were dropped before the service by my brother-in-love. I had to be back on time for our visitors. They were having the summer-out- door service at the U of T campus, with lots of fun activities and water baptisms in the near by river. The ushers were informed of my visit by my friend. They gave me a very warm welcome, calling me by my name before even introducing myself, and showed me their sincere love. I felt in my heart, that God had answered my prayers and brought me to the right place. I was seated with the family group; every single person was so loving and so welcoming. I felt accepted and loved for the first time in a church. I felt I belonged there, and I was one of them already. They were true people with genuine love. I was excited to come back again. I was introduced to the Pastor and his wife; very loving; devoted couple. I was introduced to Bible studies before I took water baptism. Two to three of the members came to my apartment, to have Bible study with me. I had to sneak out to my friend's apartment for Bible study, as my husband had not yet come to the full understanding of my new spiritual life. He still needed the time to understand. I used to get locked out at times, and was warned not to take kids with me. I never gave up praying. Glory to God, as months passed by, he started attending church with me and started reading the Bible. God has done amazing things in my life. I was free to go to church and Bible studies. We had good teachings from the Bible, but had no movements of the Holy Spirit. No one spoke in tongues. I enjoyed the teachings and fellowships. There was still a void in me. I was not sure what I was looking for. But I knew it in my heart, there was something more to it. God had not done with my search yet. I continued going to that church for almost ten years. They were one of the most loving people I met. I will never forget the love they poured into my life. I still keep in touch with few of them who are so dear to me and my family, even though I am not a member of that church anymore. Thank you so much, Delia and Yanick, for pouring your love in to my life till this very day.

Then came a time; one of my close friends from Bahrain, who had worked at the same hospital, settled in Canada, (who is gone home to be with the Lord), invited me to attend a prayer meeting in her house. I attended, and liked the way they prayed. The Pastor and few of them prayed in tongues. That was something new to me and interesting. I didn't feel strange. I felt a divine connection, although I did not speak or even attempt to speak in tongues. God was directing my paths. Very soon my husband's cousin visited us from Australia. A tongue talking spirit filled Christian. We had prayer meetings at home with her, with more deeper Bible studies. I talked to her about this new experience of mine. I took her to both these churches. Before she left, she advised me to stick to the spirit filled church. I agreed and started going to the new church. My family joined me most of the time. We were small in number. I still had fellowship with few of my friends from my previous church. They were loving people, who made me feel so much at home. I can never forget them. One day I will go back and speak to them about the goodness and kindness of God which they sowed in to my heart which was never wasted, for the glory of God. They need to know; the love that they sowed into my heart has manifested into a great harvest. They showed me the true sacrificial love of God. That will never ever be erased from my heart. I think of them often and pray for them.

My husband went back to Bahrain after a year, to visit my sister and family and our pet. What I am about to say may amaze many. Our pet dog was so happy to see his Dad. We knew he was missing us badly, even though he had no lack of love or attention. My sister used to send us pictures of him holding on to our, left behind clothes with a sad face. It used to make us feel so bad and sad. When the time was right, we wanted to bring him to Canada. We had to wait. After two weeks, it was time for my husband to return. Our pet did not let him pack. He knew he was going to be left behind again. He wanted to go with his Dad. So, he jumped inside the suitcase, and sat there. Would not budge. By force they had to take him out. He was promised, he would come home to us. He must have felt rejected and broken once again. He had tears in his eyes as at the first time. He thought his Dad had come to take him home with him. He felt deserted once again. No other love could replace his own family's love. He was broken and shattered inside. No one could understand the depth of pain he was going through. He was inactive and did not eat for few days, just as in the initial days when we left him for the first time. My sister and brother-in-love did all they could to keep him happy. They lavished him with love and catered to his favourite food and snacks every day. Polo candies (Mint candies) and eggs were his favourites. When ever I used to bring the grocery bags in, he knew exactly which bag to go for. He growled at anyone who touched his bag. If not checked, he would run with the whole bag under the bed to have a feast with his favourite candies. Even with the silver foil covering, he could eat them all. Boiled eggs, he would swallow quickly and look around as though nothing went in. He was so funny. The Middle East people didn't generally like dogs, and we had some challenges when he barked aloud. One day a neighbour complained and the police came to take him away. We were confident the police wouldn't touch him, as he would growl, and they would be afraid of him. That's exactly what happened. He growled, and they left. No further complaints. Glory to God. So many great memories of him.

A week passed after my husband returned. We were sad, after we heard of all the news of our pet. Then we received a devastating phone call from my sister. It was a real sad and bad news. He did not wake up that morning. Normally he would jump when my brother-in-love would bring his leash to take him for his morning walk. This time, he was still fast asleep in a comfortable position on his bed, so what my brother-in-love thought. It was very unusual, he would sleep that way. My brother-in-love shook him to wake him up. He was still warm but not moving or breathing. He must have taken his last breath not too long ago. They cried. They didn't want to, but had to inform us. He was probably heart broken, because his family had betrayed him twice. He could no longer handle the pain. We were devastated. Felt pain and guilt at the same time. He missed us and died heart broken. It was too much for us to handle. We did not want to tell the kids yet. They would cry badly, we knew. After some days, we slowly broke the news. It was unbearable for them. He was their triplet brother. They were devastated. We brought them a hamster to distract their pain. Gradually we overcame our grief but never forgotten him. After a year, the hamster died; everyone missed the hamster, mostly the kids, always watching him on his wheels and feeding him after school. We watched the hamster preparing the nest under the bed (News paper bed), in the cage one day. It had a big stomach. We thought it ate a lot. Didn't even know it was a female, and was pregnant from pet store itself. One day as I was driving back home from my chores, I received a frantic call from my kids, "Mamma, come soon." They were already back from school. My heart dropped. I thought some thing bad had happened to them. I asked them if they were ok, and they said "Yes." I could breathe then. They said, the hamster has babies, six of them. I asked them not to panic, not to touch them and to stay calm. I drove quickly home, and seen both the kids still around the cage. I myself did not know what to do. Sad to say, they looked ugly without the fur. I called the pet store for advice; they said after 2-3 weeks I could take them to the pet store. They would be ok with the mother until then, and I didn't have to do anything special. I was relieved. They started looking cuter as the fur began to appear. At the set time, we took the babies to the pet store, and they awarded the Mom with a bag of food. So, Mom was left alone with us. She was pampered. We didn't know if she missed them.

After the hamster days, it was sad time again. One morning we found her dead. Kids wanted a pet again. I was not very keen, because they needed our time. Kids would promise they would take care, but parents end up doing everything. At least we needed some time. Then one day, while I was asleep after night shift, my husband came in and woke me up. I thought I had slept in late. Not so. He had something tucked inside his coat, holding it with one hand. He said he had brought me something. Then he showed me something, looking like a goat. It appeared to me like a little goat. It had a long beard and fur puffed high on it's head. It didn't look anything like a dog. He said it was a puppy. I couldn't believe, until it started barking. I was happy, and the kids were happy; work was back to me again. Had to bottle feed him, and take care of him. He was growing into an adorable dog, a pincher, poodle mix, a rare type with goat's features. When his beard was trimmed he did look like a puppy. Soon he got well adapted. He is still with us after 14 years. Glory to God. A very faithful dog. His name is Rocky. He does not eat dog food, only home cooked food. All our dogs did the same. Our grand daughter loves him, and he gets so excited when ever she is around.

We were looking for jobs. Everyone asked for Canadian experience. Once I told them, how could one get any experience, unless someone allows them to work. I did not want to pursue after my nursing carrier. I felt I needed a break. I never had any experience in any other fields. Tried many, but that was not God's will. My sister-in-love once said, my resume was not tailored according to the position I applied for. I could not say anything otherwise, as I was competent only in my field. So, I gave up and decided to do the Canadian board exam. During this time, I was already working in a retirement home as a co-ordinator. With the night shift and kids, I did not get much time to study. My husband helped me a lot with house hold chores and cooking. Still not enough of time. My friends went for a preparatory course. I did not have the time. I totally relied on God. I was maturing in my faith, and asked the Holy Spirit to help me. The last few days I revised some question and answers. The same friend of mine who invited me for the prayer meeting had always encouraged me to pursue my carrier. I had more books to refer to. The day came for the exam. The exam centre was in Hamilton. A whole day's test. My husband's friend drove us early morning, straight from his night shift. We had God's favour every where. They dropped me and went back home. After the test I took the bus back. I asked God only for one thing. Let all the questions be from where I revised in the past three days. By then I knew to ask the Holy Spirit for help. The test papers were handed in. I asked the Holy Spirit to come and sit in my lap, take my pen and write my exam. He sure did. As I glanced at the exam paper, a new strength arose in me. I felt so confident. A great peace came upon the inside of me. He did exactly what I asked Him to do. Every question, came from where I had revised the previous three days. I was able to finish my test quickly, and was the first one to hand in the papers. I was so confident of my victory. God proved himself so faithful to me once again. We were told not to call, but to wait for 4-6 weeks for the results. A Pass result would come in a small envelope, in the mail, and a failed result would come in a large envelope, with the application forms to apply again for the test.

One of the most memorable, grateful days in my life came finally. My husband checked the mail always, before he went for his afternoon shift. He called me and said, there was a small envelope from the College of Nurses. With overwhelming joy, I could not speak for a moment. Then I asked him to leave it behind, and I would get it later. I had to compose myself to go get the mail. I thanked the Lord for answering my prayers. He is so faithful. Many who took the preparatory course even, couldn't make it. God's special favour was upon me. That's the only way I was able to make it. All the Glory and thanks belongs to Him. I got the courage finally to get the mail. I opened it slowly, pulled out the paper gradually, and seen, "Passed." I wanted to scream with joy. But had to wait until I got back in to the apartment. All I could do was fall prostrate on the floor and thank my God. He did it again !!!. I remained on the floor for a while, then got up, and seen the full paper. I couldn't contain my joy. I was so happy. I called my husband and friend, and let them rejoice with me. My husband knew already. They were so happy for me. I am thankful for my friend, who always encouraged me to do the exam and get my licence to practice nursing back again. She is gone home to be with The Lord. A sincere friend who encouraged me a lot. She will never be forgotten. She put so much pressure on me until I got my licence, which brought me greater blessings, with a better job and a better salary. She is the one who invited me for prayer meeting in her home, where the tongue talking preacher and group prayed. I am so thankful to God for my husband, who was so patient with me and did all the house hold chores and cooking great meals for the family. Its amazing to see how God orchestrates our lives. Step by step He carries us to our destiny, even when we want to disobey. His ways are so marvelous. His ways are so wonderful.

I started back my career. Enjoyed my career of caring as always. My clients (Patients) were always happy with my care. God had anointed me for that job, and I was trying to run away from it. He will always bring us back to where He wants us to be. Glory to God. Challenges came when I had to do shift work and Sundays alternating. I was not happy to miss church on Sundays and midweek. I started praying to God again. I needed a job from Monday to Friday with only day shifts, so, will not have to miss church. But had no hopes in my heart to find a suitable one in my profession. To me that was unheard of. One day, when I went to work, my friend said, "Phyllis, there is a doctor hiring registered nurses for his private clinic. No shift work, and Monday to Friday, with all the weekends and statutory holidays off." That was again an answer to my prayer. I was delighted, although the pay was a little less. I was just happy not to miss church. I applied, asking God's guidance again. I said, Lord, "I am going to apply, for this post, and if its not from you, don't let them call me for an interview, and if they call me, I know its from you." They did call me for an interview. I approached God again and said, "don't let them give me the job, if its not from you." They called and gave me the orientation dates. I was so happy. To have a normal life again. My husband and kids were always used to a uniform wife and mother at any parties or family gatherings. Either I was going to work or back from a shift work. This was the most exciting time in my work history, ever since I started my family. My husband and children could finally see me around in decent hours. God gave me the best co-workers. We had so much fun together. Most of them were younger in age than I was, and I was kind of Mamma to them. There was no stress, just joyful work environment. For the first time, I started enjoying weekends and other holidays with my family. It was so refreshing and gratifying. Years went by. I enjoyed my family, my church, and my work. God always granted me the desires of my heart and never withheld the requests of my lips. What an awesome God we serve.

Life had many roller coasters. Each time, God brought us forth stronger. The year 2007, was again to face with sadness. My husband's younger sister went home to be with the Lord. She was the family's net worker. Kept everyone together. We miss her a lot. Several years ago, my husband's older brother as well went home to be with the Lord.

The year 2006, brought a great answer to my decades of prayer. It was time for my vision test. Sure enough, more expenses, I thought. My eye glasses needed to be changed. Since it had added comfort features, it was expensive. The doctor also mentioned, that there was cataract forming in my eyes, and that I should wait until it matures to undergo surgery. So, I had to wait for my new glasses. My vision was getting dimmer. The same time, I was facing some gynaecological problems as well, which needed attention. The doctor had warned me that my life was at risk without a hysterectomy, because of excessive bleeding with fibroids. My haemoglobin was so low, I used to feel dizzy all the time, and had no energy at all. To live without the Word is so dangerous. All I knew was to accept doctors report and go by their advice. Never knew to speak the Word over my situations at that time. By the year 2010, I became more mature spiritually. The date for surgery was fixed. First hysterectomy, then surgery for cataract to follow, in two weeks. I was overwhelmed with fear of surgery. Fear of not waking up from anaesthesia. I remember, talking to my cousin, about my important documents; where they were kept, in case I didn't wake up from anaesthesia. My husband was never interested in documents and files. My kids were still young. We do foolish things with fear. Glory to God, I had a safe surgery. In two weeks time, both my cataracts were out, with lens implantation. This was like the 2nd miracle in my personal life. Post surgery check up in the clinic was appointed. The bandage on my eye was removed. Lo and behold, I could see so well without glasses, for which I had prayed for decades. The devil thought he could blind me with cataract. God turned it around for my good. I was so happy, I could dance around the street. I could only thank The Lord for His miraculous blessing.

In 2009, tragedy struck again. My husband's Mom, (my mother-in-love), went home to be with the Lord. She was more than a mother to me. A very loving, kind, and no faultfinding Mom, specially when it comes to her daughter-in-loves. She would correct her sons instead, and instruct them to take good care of their wives. My husband was rebuked by her many times when ever he got distracted from taking responsibility. I was very blessed to have her in my life. God is so good, He gave me loving parents and siblings; and again, put me in to another loving family. God blessed me with a loving husband, loving in-laws, loving children and loving grand children. I am a blessed woman. Glory to God. When I count all my blessings, there is no room for complaints. I am not perfect, sometimes when pressure mounts with challenges, I do complain, then again I repent and get back to normal. God's Word is teaching me to be quick to forgive and walk in love, with no place for offence or strife. I am learning to walk in forgiveness and in love. With Holy Spirit's strength, I am able to do it.

2012 was unfolding with challenges again. The enemy was trying to steal my life once again. One night, I picked up my husband from work, and as we were exiting the high way to our home, a lady ran the red light and hit our car. We went in circles in a shattered car. It was terrible. I tried to steer the car to no effect. The impact was so bad, it made circles and went to the opposite direction. The air bags were out, and smoke came out. I was afraid, the car would go in to flames. It took me a while to get my seatbelt off. My husband got out first, and made sure I was ok, then I got out, just limping. We sat at the pavement just trying to gather ourselves while a good Samaritan called for the ambulance. The truck which hit us was stationed on the pavement, with the occupants sitting not far from us. The Passenger in that truck had the nerve to tell me why I did that. She thought she could accuse me and get away. Many witnesses came forward and gave report to the police. This, one particular young man; thanks, be unto him forever, who was just behind our car, had watched me exiting on green light, and had also seen, how this lady ran the red light and hit us. He stayed back and gave all the reports to the police and was willing to testify against my accuser. We were transported to the nearby hospital in the ambulance. Our kids had already arrived at the scene. We were seen by the doctors, all required tests were performed. No broken bones, but very sore. We were bruised in our bodies, more to the right side of my body, from hip to the toes. It turned purple black. Had difficulty in walking. We were sent home after few hours of observation, with pain medications, to be followed up by the family doctor. While we were at the hospital, the police visited, and gave us the report. He said that I was not at fault. And the driver in the other vehicle would never drive again, as she already had many convictions, and her licence to drive was already removed. No weapon formed against the children of God shall prosper. Thanks, be unto God. He rescued our lives, and put the false accusers in their place. We recovered slowly, with physiotherapies and so on. One more bitter experience arose after 2 years; while I was coming out of all the trauma of this incident. This same lady through her lawyer wanted to take me to court, suing me over Million dollars for the bodily harm she endured due to the accident, which was in fact caused by her own friend's reckless and careless driving. This lady was the passenger of that vehicle. I checked with my lawyer, and only then I came to know that, such law existed, that the passenger of the vehicle could sue the driver, even if its not the driver's fault. I was distraught, angry and upset. I said to myself; her careless friend should have been sued instead, for causing such harm to me, not just physically, but emotionally and financially. I am not happy to mention what happened then, but I have to, only to let others know, how God takes care of His children. At the given court date, I appeared with my lawyer. Both the lawyers spoke for a while, before they allowed me to join them.

My accuser was absent. Her lawyer spoke to me and asked further questions and filled out more papers. There was no change in my statement even after 2 years. He said, the case was dismissed, and I was free to leave. I was not sure as to what was happening, and did not understand exactly what was going on. I looked at my lawyer, for some explanation. She said she would explain to me privately. I was taken to another room and given the explanation. She said, my accuser was terminally ill with cancer, and that was the reason of her absence, and she was not able to or wanting to pursue after me anymore. Although I was thankful to God for lifting my burden and rescuing me, I was not happy with this sad news. I felt sad, and asked if I could speak to her and pray with her. Because it was a legal matter, it was not possible. I prayed for that woman, that God would heal her. I asked the lawyer to let her know that I have forgiven her and have nothing against her. I have experienced many times, God's saving hands over me. He takes good care of His sheep. I remember going to my Minister in the church, Minister Cheryl, my Pastor's wife, to pray about this situation. I will never forget the comfort I received from her through God's Words. I am so thankful to God for my Pastor; Pastor John Ward and his beautiful wife, Minister Cheryl. They are such great Godly examples to us. They don't just teach us the Word, but they live the Word; and are always willing and ready to help us. Thank you, Pastor Ward and Minister Cheryl, for raising me up to this level, spiritually. I have learned so much from both of you. You are one of my answered prayers. God put me in the right church with you.

Back to my recovery. Months went by with physiotherapies

and legal appointments. Was away from work for a very long time. Decided to go to India for further treatment, with natural medicines. In the mean time, we got the news that my Dad was not feeling that well. God's timing was perfect. Children and I went first, followed by my husband. Dad was diagnosed with lung cancer. It was devastating. Only palliative care with pain medications were prescribed. We stood in faith, and believed for his recovery. He was actively taking care of the church which my sister and brother-in-love had planted, while still in Bahrain. The enemy had a hard time to bear that. Close to 90, still knocking at doors to bring people to church. The enemy wanted to stop him from doing God's work. He was in lot of pain, unable to walk without assistance, as the whole body was affected by then. I was not able to pay much attention to myself. But did see the naturopathic doctor and took medications. I was recovering, but had to take more time. It was Christmas time, and Dad's 90th birthday was approaching as well. All the family and friends wanted a grant party for him. Our kids were not able to wait, so both of them flew back to Canada. Dad celebrated his 90th birthday very grant, with all his family and friends. It was his last birthday on earth. All were around him except he missed our kids. He was very understanding; that they needed to go. Alston, one of our twins was not very well when he left. I trusted God he would soon feel better. Then came a frantic call one early morning, that he had seizures. He was taken to hospital, and later sent home. Aldon, his brother was with him. I was shattered again. Who to be with? Dad or my son? Since all my siblings and family were with Dad, I didn't want my child to be left unattended. So, we booked our flights back to Toronto. Was sad to leave Dad, but happy to be with our children. Thanks be to God, all reports, including the CT scan were normal. God's mighty saving hands were always with us. I had plans to return to Dad after some time, to be with him as well to continue with my treatment. Just two days passed. On the 3rd day after we arrived, my sister called me, sobbing. I knew without explanation. Then she completed her sentence. Alston said I should not have come back. How can he know a mother's heart. He said he would buy me the ticket to go back for my Dad's funeral. I prayed about it and decided not to go. Kids had already helped us much for our first trip. Except us, the rest were present at his funeral. Perhaps my Dad was just waiting to see my kids. He had not seen them for 18 years, and always had cried over the phone, wanting to see them. My husband and I had visited him in between. He would ask my kids to sit on his bed and would listen to their stories. God granted him the desires of his heart, before he went home to be with the Lord. God's strength was sufficient enough to take us through our tragedies.

Years were moving faster. Our family started growing. One of our twins, (Aldon), got settled with his life partner, our daughter-in-love, Marnelli. Then came our most precious addition. Our precious grand daughter Ariana. The joy of our lives. The Apple of our eyes. The Treasure of our hearts. This precious gift came straight from heaven. She was born on August 8th, 2014; Just three months after I started writing this book. I definitely had to put away my book writing. It took me a long time to catch up again. Now, we have become the proud grand parents. Glory to God. What a promotion in our lives. We cherished every moment with her. She brought such joy and happiness in our lives, we couldn't contain. Many said she looks like her grandma. As she is growing, she is bringing so much joy in our lives. She loves to sing, and dance. She was interested in ipad and cell phones from an early age. Becoming grand parent is a totally different experience. 2016 blessed us with more addition to our family. Our grandson of 15 years, arrived from the Philippines. A great and wonderful kid, God's precious gift again. He adjusted well with us. We became one big happy family. Waiting for our next twin in line, (Alston), to add his supply. In God's own time, He will perfect everything. All the praises and glory belongs to our God. 2014 was the most spectacular; the most memorable; and the most remarkable year in my life. Our precious grand daughter arrived that year, visited Israel with my brother and family, attended brother Copeland's convention, and was placed in the right church by God where I am enjoying my life till this day. It was indeed a spectacular year in my life. One glory time after the other. I cannot thank God enough for all of His Blessings.

I am a blessed woman. A blessed daughter, a blessed sister, a blessed wife, a blessed mother, a blessed grandmother, and a blessed friend. I am so blessed to see my children and grandchildren prospering. I immerse my family in prayer every day and speak God's Word over their lives. I declare daily that my seed (children) are mighty on earth, the generation of the upright are blessed, wealth and riches are in my house and my righteousness endures forever (Psalm 112:2-3), and much more Scriptures. God is bringing to pass every desire of my heart. Glory to God.

I decided to quit my Job. God was directing me into some

other path. I was already in a spirit filled church since 2014. How did I get here? Its another story. The pastor of my small church had to leave for the Middle East, to establish further with his brother. A new pastor with his wife, (Both were Pastors) took over our church. We were well taken care, spiritually. They taught us about faith and all the biblical principles. They taught us from the teachings of Copland's and like wise spirit filled teachers. They were older couples, but had great energy and passion for the Lord. I was still looking out for something. Few who knew to speak in tongues, prayed silently. I wanted to see the move. I approached the pastor and expressed what I was looking for. She said she would help me with it. I was going through some spiritual struggles. I knew I needed more. I loved my pastors and did not want to leave the 2nd church. It was one big challenge to come out of my first church, trying to root myself in the right church, pulling my family along. It was not spiritual fun time for me. If my family had the understanding to what I was looking for, it would have been much easier. I had to stand strong amidst all the criticism. I was sad at times and confused at times. One day I spoke to the Holy Spirit and asked for help. I asked Him to send me to a spirit filled church, where I can experience the move of the Spirit. I also said, I needed guidance in my decision to leave this church, as I didn't want to hurt my pastors. The Holy Spirit was not against my desires. He clearly spoke to me, even with an audible voice. He said, "go speak to your pastor." It was so clear, I didn't have to struggle any more. So, I gathered myself and called my pastor and said I wanted to speak to them. At the given time, I met them. (Both were pastors). All through my travel time to meet them, I prayed, "Holy Spirit, please speak through my mouth, and let no unwanted word come out of my mouth." The Holy Spirit helped me to speak. He gave me the courage. I was not nervous anymore. I looked straight into their eyes, and said, I want to grow more spiritually, and to please bless me and release me, and that I am sorry for hurting them. My pastor was silent. His wife spoke. She said, "of course Phyllis, we will not be hurt, but would bless you and release you." I felt a heavy burden lifted off of me. I was happy to hear they will not be hurt. That was my only concern. My pastor asked me if I knew any churches. I said no. I asked him if he could suggest me. He gave me the names of two churches. One was Word of Faith on Victoria park and O'Conner, and the next was Destiny and Dominion. I did visit Destiny and Dominion when brother Jerry Saville was visiting. Word of Faith was closer. So, I decided to attend Word of Faith. I had visited this church twice when Pastor Terry Copeland came to Toronto. I didn't know God was all the while directing me here. Many historical events happened in my life in 2014. Finally, I found what I was looking for. God knew my heart's desires and placed me in the right place. I am so blessed with my Pastor and family of God here. I started my new spiritual journey; started attending Word of faith church since 1st October 2014. During the membership class, I remember asking the Minister, if they taught like the Copeland's. I didn't want to be in the wrong place any more. I had wasted much time. I was reassured. I was so happy. Finally, I can learn and grow spiritually, which is what God is doing in my life. I wanted to join the bible school immediately. I was late. Classes had already started in September. I didn't want to miss out on the next enrollment. Glory to God, He put me in Bible school, and blessed me with much. I was graduated from the Bible School on 29th of June 2018. All the glory, honor and thanks belongs to our God. Without Him, I would not have made it. In fact I would have been dead long back. I went to Bible School, thinking, I am just going to learn the Bible more deeply. Little did I know, there was more to it. I was challenged with many subjects and home work on the computer which was not my favourite part. Initially, thought of quitting. But the wonderful support and love given by our Dean and teacher Minister Cheryl, our Pastor and all our teachers, kept me going forward. The Holy Spirit and all of them held my back and brought me to the finish line. I am confident, God will raise me up to all what He wants me to be, as a great witness to the gospel.

I am thankful to God, for my husband, my children and grand children for all their sacrifices, love, and support. My husband always had helped me with house hold chores specially cooking, which is not my passion. I want them to know how much I love them and cherish them and how grateful I am to God for them. I may not have expressed my gratitude and love for them always. But without them I would never have come this far. There were times in my life, when I had missed seeing those blessings. But I had repented always, when ever my heart turned ungrateful towards God. Family is a true Blessing from God. I am so Blessed with my family. Thanks to my parents who taught me the great values of family. I am especially thankful to my daughter-in-love Marnelli who helped me with my lap top to do my first home work in Bible school.

Thanks to her loving heart. Above all I am thankful to God for her for carrying both my precious grand children. I am also thankful to both my sons, daughter-in-love, and grandson, who helped me with my print outs and computer work. My precious grand daughter who had not started school yet then, wanted to teach me as well. She is an expert on her ipad, who knows more than her grandmother.

I love my church family as well. I am so blessed with our Pastor, and his wife, (our Minister), who showers us with so much love. They are such great examples to us. They are always there for us. They just don't preach and teach. They do the work. I have grown so much spiritually here. I love the rest of my spiritual family as well.

From 2009, I was recognising the changes in me. I wanted no more to be a party girl which I had become with my husband. My upbringing was different. My parents and siblings never drank or partied. They were sober people. We did have family get-togethers. I was exposed to a different life-style, which I had enjoyed as well. I remember my party days, with my husband and family, which ended in the early morning hours. Went home after party, took a shower, took black coffee, put on my uniform, and went off to work. I could go sleepless for many days. Foolish days with no wisdom of God. 2010 was a year with some wisdom. My husband had lost his job. I was not anxious. But it was time, to keep our finances in order. Parties do cost money. So, I spoke to my husband and said, "we need to make some adjustments, now that we are with one income." I said I was not going for regular parties anymore, neither having one at home. All are welcome anytime, and I will be glad to share what I have at home." He did not disagree, although I knew he would miss it. It was about time to start making the adjustments. All things work together for good, to those who love God, to those who are the called, according to His purpose. Glory to God. We did attend important functions. This new decision gave me some physical and financial rest. I thank the Lord for His Wisdom.

Attending a convention at the Copeland's in 2013, was the first time, my spiritual eyes got opened. I knew there is more in store for me in the Kingdom. I learned in a very deep way about the principle of sowing and reaping. I learned the importance of tithing. I knew I had to obey what God's Word says, in order to reap the harvest of my blessing. I had to learn how to speak in line with His Words. This mess we landed in is, just the outcome of our wrong choices, and the wrong words coming out of our mouths, and from other's mouths, spoken over us. Wow!!! Wow!!! Wow!!!; ignorance can really kill us. The Bible says so. People perish due to lack of knowledge. So true. Thank God for His Mercy and Grace. He is so faithful and patient with us.

It was very clear, there was no other way around. I had tried many other ways before. It didn't bring me true prosperity. My sister who knew the Lord before me, used to talk to me about tithing. I said to her, "you have no idea what you are talking about. Its not the Middle East, its Canada. You find only bills here." I just ignored her advice. Didn't pay any attention to it. I never knew the principle of tithing until I went to brother Copeland's meeting. I had heard about it in my previous church, my sister had mentioned about it many times, but I had no understanding of the principle.

In our early days in Canada, we had faced some financial challenges. We didn't know, how to balance our new lives. We had to learn the hard way. We were never used to credit cards. Without even requesting, they started appearing in the mail, just on time. Specially Christmas time, when the expenses were so high. We thought it came as a blessing on time. I didn't know it was devil's deception. It took me a while to recognize it and our finances got into a bit of mess. By then I had learned, that God's way was the only way to get out of the mess I got in without him. I sought the Lord's guidance, started putting His Word in to action, followed the prosperity principles of the Bible, and not very long, I was out of debt. My way of thinking before was, that a Christian should not be rich, should not possess material goods, and should only barely get by; and that was humility to me. Little did I know that it was satan's lies from the pit of hell. Now I think the opposite. Glory to God, for that great revelation knowledge. Our Father in heaven is a rich Daddy. Everything belongs to Him. We his children are heirs to His wealth, being co-heirs with Christ. Barely getting by is a sin, because we are not operating in His principles. It applies in all areas of our lives. Health, Peace, joy, Marriage, Finances, and everything. In Him we have everything. When the enemy comes in like a flood, the Spirit of The Lord will lift up a standard against him. We are covered by His Precious Blood. The evil enemy cannot touch us, unless we let him. Challenges will come. The devil is already a defeated foe. We don't need to fight our battle. Our battle is already won. We are victorious, more than conquerors. We just need to remind the devil, and put him in his place. We have the power and authority over him. There is power in that name; The Name of Jesus. The greater one, His Holy Spirit lives inside of us. We are his power house. Just plug in, and that power will show up itself. It works like the dynamite. The dunamis power of the Holy Spirit. Thank You God, for The Holy Spirit.

As I am maturing in Christ; I am learning so much about the Kingdom principles. Learning to depend on God for everything. Phyllis is not her boss anymore. Jesus is her Boss. I have learned to yield to the Holy Spirit, in all my ways. I still make mistakes. But I am quick to repent and make the adjustments. I like the way our pastor teaches us. He tells us, "don't condemn yourself when you make a mistake, just repent and make the adjustments." He makes it so easy for us. God bless our Pastor and Minister Cheryl. Always encouraging and supporting us, teaching us the right thing. I am learning to quickly forgive as well. Strife, offence, unforgiveness and judging others, will not hinder my blessings anymore. That curse is broken already. I don't carry that bondage anymore, but walk in total freedom now; casting all my cares unto Him. I walk in victory and peace, knowing I am well taken care of. The joy of the Lord is my strength. I can laugh at the devil boldly; Ha..Ha.. Ha, like our pastor taught us.

I am learning to get into that deeper walk with God. Living by faith and walking in love. We are taught to obey His commandments and walk in His blessings. Thanks to the wonderful teachings we receive in our church. Speaking God's Words over our lives and our situations are so important; I have learned. Words are spirit. They have power. They are containers. Death and life are in the power of our tongue; the Bible says so. We can have what we say. Good or bad. Only we, can control our tongues; no one else. Likewise, we cannot control other's tongues either. I am learning to speak with discernment and receive with discernment. I do make mistakes at times. God's grace abounds in me. I am still under construction. People will remind you of your mistakes, specially the ones who know you closer. But Thanks be to God's wisdom and knowledge. No more guilt and shame. His Blood has washed me and cleansed me from all unrighteousness. He looks at me as sin never existed in me. What a privilege to be in His Kingdom. Glory to God.

This new life has brought, tremendous peace and joy in to my life. I am enjoying every minute of it until Jesus returns. It is my earnest desire to have a closer walk with God, continue to do His will, and serve Him with honesty, integrity and excellence, for the rest of my life. The good work what He started in me, He will complete, until Jesus returns. To God alone be all the Glory, all the Honor, and all the Praises.

I want to express my gratitude to some of my close friends of many years in the kingdom, who poured out their love, and contributed so much in to my life. Thank you once again, Delia, Yanick and family, for all that you did for me, and all that you are to me, from the time I touched my feet in this beautiful land of Canada. You stood by me, encouraged me, and supported me all the way through. You showed me God's unconditional love since the time I met you. Thank you, Mamma Margaret, Concey,

Heidi, and Lita, for always being there for me. Thank you, for your unconditional love, encouragement and support you always gave me. Mamma Margaret you are more than a Mother to me. Your strong faith in the Lord is so encouraging. Concey and kids, you have contributed much to my life. Heidi and Lita you are my cheer leaders. Always encouraging me and standing with me. I also want to express my gratitude to all the Ministers at my church who lavished me always with love and guidance. Thank you for teaching me, encouraging me, supporting me and helping me grow in the kingdom. Thank you for all that you have done for me and my family. Thank you, my congregants, for letting me enjoy life with you in the kingdom. My above and beyond gratitude goes to my Pastor, Pastor John Ward, and his precious and beautiful wife, our Minister Cheryl, who are irreplaceable. They are God's precious gifts to us. Thank you, for all that you are to us and all that you do for us. My family and I appreciate you very much. You are such a great example for each of us. Thank you for teaching and molding us to all that God wants us to be.

I Praise You, Worship You, and Thank You; Oh Lord, my King, my Master and my Saviour. You are so great; so wonderful; and so marvelous. Ever faithful, and never changing. All that I am today is; all because of you. I am nothing without you. Thank you, for picking me from the dirt, washing me, cleansing me, moulding me, and making me your child. Thank you, for the freedom; that limitless freedom, that I can come to you at any time; because you are my Daddy; my Father. You sent Jesus on the cross to save me. Your love is so amazing. Where can I find such love?. Nothing can repay that love. You removed all the fears and uncertainties from me, and gave me hope and a future. You forgave me, and lavished me with your love. You blessed me beyond my wildest dreams. When all hopes faded, disappointments mounted, when I was discouraged, when I felt lonely and alone, when others ridiculed, when I felt betrayed, when I was misunderstood, when I was pushed to the side roads, when I was not important, when I was cursed, when I was broke, and broken, when I was sick, when I was in pain, and when I was crushed; you did not leave me, nor forsake me. You stood along with me, and carried me through. You carried me through the fire and the flood. You did not let the flames touch me, nor allow the floods to drown me. You are my shield, my glory, and the lifter up of my head. You are the pillar of my life, my anchor, and the shelter of my refuge. I love you with all of my heart, with all of my strength, and all of my being. I know you have great plans for my future. You see my end from the beginning. As I trust in you, and abide in you, you will unfold my life to the destiny you have for me. With your strength, I will do all the things you want me to do. And you will supply all my needs. You are able to do exceeding abundantly above all I can ask or think, according to your power that is working in me. I am your covenant child. All that you have for me; I receive; by faith, and give you all the Glory and Thanks. As I step in to this new Glory Life, I draw my strength from you. You will lead me and guide me. Lord, I give you my word. I will become all that you want me to be, excelling in the Kingdom, for your glory. I thank you, Holy

Spirit, for helping me write my story for your Glory. I humble myself before you, and commit my life to you. Here I am!!!; use me; for your Glory. As for me and my house, we will serve you, oh Lord. To you alone be all the Glory, all the praises, all the Honor and all the Thanks; forever and ever; Amen !!!.

A SPECIAL NOTE OF THANKS

I will not be able to forward my book to the publishing company without thanking my niece and nephew who recently arrived from India. There were protocols to follow, and because of challenges with computer to follow through, I was praying and asking God to send me help. As always God did answer my prayer and sent these two kids to live with me. What a blessing they are to me. They helped me so much with my book, putting things together, and in order, specially uploading them to forward it to my publishing company. I was finally able to accomplish this long awaited task. God is always on time. He sent me help just on time.

Thanks to you, Valerine and Allan, for sacrificially giving me your time. I thank the Lord for you. Your harvest for this seed is coming to you soon. God Bless you.

Your Aunt,
Phyllis.

A SPECIAL NOTE OF THANKS

This special note of thanks goes to WestBow press, all the departments and it's associates, co-ordinators and each and every person at the WestBow press who helped me along the way, in putting this book together and fulfilling the desire of my heart. Thank you for all your help, support and encouragement you gave me from the beginning to the end. I admire your patience with me and I thank the Lord for you. I want to also thank Getty Images for providing me with a free image for my book cover.

With much appreciation and gratitude,

Phyllis Fernandez.

Printed in the United States
By Bookmasters